Koehler Briceño

Latino Farmworkers in North Carolina

Processes of Creating, Maintaining, and Believing in "Home"

Scholars Press

Impressum / Imprint

Bibliografische Information der Deutschen Nationalbibliothek: Die Deutsche Nationalbibliothek verzeichnet diese Publikation in der Deutschen Nationalbibliografie; detaillierte bibliografische Daten sind im Internet über http://dnb.d-nb.de abrufbar.

Alle in diesem Buch genannten Marken und Produktnamen unterliegen warenzeichen-, marken- oder patentrechtlichem Schutz bzw. sind Warenzeichen oder eingetragene Warenzeichen der jeweiligen Inhaber. Die Wiedergabe von Marken, Produktnamen, Gebrauchsnamen, Handelsnamen, Warenbezeichnungen u.s.w. in diesem Werk berechtigt auch ohne besondere Kennzeichnung nicht zu der Annahme, dass solche Namen im Sinne der Warenzeichen- und Markenschutzgesetzgebung als frei zu betrachten wären und daher von jedermann benutzt werden dürften.

Bibliographic information published by the Deutsche Nationalbibliothek: The Deutsche Nationalbibliothek lists this publication in the Deutsche Nationalbibliografie; detailed bibliographic data are available in the Internet at http://dnb.d-nb.de.

Any brand names and product names mentioned in this book are subject to trademark, brand or patent protection and are trademarks or registered trademarks of their respective holders. The use of brand names, product names, common names, trade names, product descriptions etc. even without a particular marking in this work is in no way to be construed to mean that such names may be regarded as unrestricted in respect of trademark and brand protection legislation and could thus be used by anyone.

Coverbild / Cover image: www.ingimage.com

Verlag / Publisher:
Scholar's Press
ist ein Imprint der / is a trademark of
OmniScriptum GmbH & Co. KG
Bahnhofstraße 28, 66111 Saarbrücken, Deutschland / Germany
Email: info@omniscriptum.com

Herstellung: siehe letzte Seite /
Printed at: see last page
ISBN: 978-3-639-71882-9

Copyright © 2014 OmniScriptum GmbH & Co. KG
Alle Rechte vorbehalten. / All rights reserved. Saarbrücken 2014

Table of Contents

Acknowledgements

I would like to thank Doctor Peacock for all of the aid and encouragement that he has provided me throughout this entire thesis process. I could not have accomplished a fraction of what I have achieved without his optimism, holistic knowledge, or friendship.

I would like to thank Professor Patricia Sawin for the assistance in fine-tuning techniques that she offered to me, as well as ways to broaden my scope and heighten the impact of my finished product. I appreciate the time and effort that Professor Hannah Gill and Luis Marcelino Gómez dedicated to the development of my thesis as well.

I would like to thank the Anthropology Honors Thesis Class of 2008-2009 for the friendship and solidarity they offered to me through their encouragements, constructive criticisms, questions, answers, and cheese fries. Thanks to Meg Kassabaum and her guidance and strength as she steered her fledgling undergraduate anthropologists towards our goals.

I would like to thank Student Action with Farmworkers, Alianza, Coalition for College Access, Christian Ministry for Farmworkers, and all other individuals and organizations that have generated and nurtured my passion for Latino and immigrant issues.

Lastly, I would like to thank Father Rafa, Elias, Fito, Arturo, and Rudolfo (whose story and friendship are equally valued although it is not present in my thesis) for allowing me a glimpse at their lives, hopes, dreams, passions, and goals for the future; for helping me to understand "home" in North Carolina.

Dedication

I dedicate my thesis to my family: my dad, mom, brother, grandparents, aunts, uncles, cousins, and friends. Without their cradle of love, acceptance, and stability I would be lost. They are my rock, my comfort, my home.

Introduction

Why I chose this topic

Why, with the multitude of destinations made increasingly accessible by our globalized world, do people choose to live where they do? Larger forces –economic pressures, family responsibility, social or environmental crisis –may displace people from their original place of residence, but ultimately they make the decision about where to settle and develop a future, create a home. I still do not presume to understand how people generally choose where they best "fit," because I realize that, as one of my interviewees Elias says, "Each head is a different world; the way he thinks is different." Acknowledging the innumerous possibilities of human orientation towards a place also requires the acceptance of diverging sets of desires and reactions to challenging or supportive opportunities and environments. North Carolina experienced a 273.7% growth in foreign-born populations between 1990 and 2000, making it the state with the highest percentage increase in the United States; additionally, it claims the sixth largest population of farmworkers within the U.S. (US Census, SAF fact sheet 2007[1]). The 2000-2001 National Agricultural Workers Survey (NAWS) documented that 82% of farmworkers self-identified as Hispanic, whereas 72% additionally labeled themselves as Mexican (2005). I chose to seek an answer for why and how Latino immigrant farmworkers make North Carolina their home. The attraction and pull for foreign-born populations to the state into which I have plunged my own roots intrigued me, especially given the dynamic controversy over their intentions, rights, and belonging that has captured political public attention, and my own family history.

My father emigrated from Bolivia to the United States at the age of 19, and Washington D.C. has been his "home" ever since. Knowing my dad, I recognize that his decisions are firm, pre-meditated, and permanent; however, I still question *why* he chose to invest his effort in creating a future, livelihood, and home within a nation that separated him from his childhood memories, five siblings (an additional sister was pre-established in the U.S.), and basically the only culture and way of life that he had previously known. His migration occurred during the presidency of Jimmy Carter, when Latino immigrants found it

---

[1] The Student Action with Farmworkers (SAF) website has data sheets with compiled information concerning farmworkers in North Carolina and the U.S.; these helped me profoundly in locating government censes and informational websites to expound my research on current Latino immigrant and farmworker statistics.

much easier to receive visas. However, the flow of immigration since the seventies has increased exponentially, despite the U.S.'s discouraging political and social response. The new incorporation of rural towns and Southeastern areas within the past ten years' focus of immigrant flow stimulates a constant stream of questioning as to why and how immigrants choose the place to establish a future, a home.

Regarding the 21st century crescendo of Latino immigrant presence within North Carolina, I acknowledge that new arrivals' initial interest is most likely due to employment opportunity. North Carolina, because of present and historic economic alignments, provides bountiful low-wage labor jobs in two sectors: construction jobs in prospering, growing, town/cities such as Greensboro, Raleigh, etcetera; and agricultural jobs predominantly in the Eastern piedmont. Agriculture interested me for two reasons: primarily, it was more feasible for me to get in contact with agricultural workers and participants of that realm of North Carolina society; and secondly, its seasonal nature. Unlike immigrants employed within (more) urban areas, farmworkers are constricted by the nature of their job, which situates them in rural areas, and usually requires them to live in a "camp" that is near if not on the fields in which they work. Since the demand for farmworkers changes with the harvest season, it is not a guaranteed yearlong position, and therefore settlement and residence are not encouraged by this occupation, specifically. Additionally, the H-2A "guestworker" seasonal visas that are offered to migrant agricultural laborers are contingent on the individual's agreement to return to their country of origin after the seasonal term of employment. Therefore, I hypothesized that agricultural workers' decision to stay in North Carolina was more complex than simple economic incentives and that there was a process of attachment and forging of connections that allowed a farmworker to begin to consider this state as their home.

Migrant farmworkers of North Carolina, generally speaking, face an environment of indifference if not hostilities that "center on the idea of cultural confrontation and identity" (Daniel Arreola 2004:33). Agricultural laborers' silent contributions to the U.S. are widely unacknowledged and the workers themselves are commonly met with condemnation because of negative attitudes towards the overall Latino presence in the U.S. that result from threatened identity. I knew, from my own timid involvement, that in addition to opposition, organizations in defense and support of farmworker and immigrant rights have blossomed throughout North Carolina, not only drawing attention and concern for their politically unacknowledged voice, but also supporting and empowering them to, "make noise, yell, cry: noise" (Father Rafa interview). I originally wanted to interview individuals that covered every angle of a migrant farmworker's social interaction with North Carolina in order to comprehend holistically the process of finding balance between hostile and welcoming environments. However, I realized that the relationship between farmworkers and aid agencies was the most intimate and purposeful, and would consequentially provide the deepest introspection into farmworker interactions within North Carolina. Further, I eventually found a solid network of political, economic, and social aid that emanated from a single fount, the Christian Ministry for Farmworkers (CMFF), which served as the uniting axle of my three case studies.

My thesis demonstrates that political and social policies and attitudes towards Latino populations ensure preemptive judgment by the general public in the hopes of dissuading immigrants' creation of home within the USA. However, immigrants' determination to struggle against the hostile domestic ambience reaffirms their genuine hopes to better their future at the cost of no one except for perhaps their own present selves, yet this is a sacrifice they willingly undergo. Farmworkers stoically negate and strip away the assigned identity of the sterilized, stereotypical, "Mexican," "illegal," "immigrant," and demand identity through "senses and beliefs of belonging that determine their everyday actions and practices " of creating a home (Alejandra Castañeda 2006:3).

Through my fieldwork, I identified three dimensions of finding or establishing a home for North Carolina farmworkers. "Home" is individually interpreted and defined; however, temporal and inside/outside alignments create conceptual pools of understanding what, how, and who "home" encompasses. Home can be memories of the past, optimistic goals for the future, or present senses of belonging, purpose, and community. Additionally, "home" feelings are stimulated by both internal and external factors. Community, family, social environments, these create and challenge opportunities to feel "at home," on a level outside of the self. However, regarding home as a dream or goal of the past or future is primarily internal. Whether an individual is oriented towards the past or future, internally or externally driven to decide upon a place to call home, I perceive the *need* to establish a home as inevitable. Therefore, the desire and drive to create a home, whether it be temporary, permanent, emotional, spiritual, or a physical structure, is an underlying vein that not only surges through my case studies, but all individuals and levels of society as well.

Fito, Arturo, Father Rafa, and Elias all expressed the idea of "home" as a prospect for the future, usually within North Carolina, and a motivation to endure the present through their narratives. Other variations include "home" as an idealized, cherished, memory including the country of origin; this "home" also encourages farmworkers to persevere through their present, immediate, struggles, with emphasis on *returning* to their home (in their country of origin) rather than working to *create* a new one. The third concept of home can coexist within the hearts of farmworkers alongside either of the first two, and is what aid agencies such as CMFF hope to provide through their efforts to support, protect, and improve farmworkers' present experiences within North Carolina. The availability of the third home sentiment is contingent upon feeling welcomed, belonging to a community or family, being visible and acknowledged within different levels of society, supporting oneself, and having agency. In order to illustrate the challenges that aid agencies and farmworkers battle with to feel "at home" within North Carolina, I have emphasized the importance of living and working conditions, empowerment, and social justice, within my case studies section.

Purpose and Methodology

In the quest to understand the emotional, social, political, and environmental dynamics that accompany migrant farmworkers' decision to make a home in North Carolina, I balanced my research between fieldwork and scholarly sources. My motive in doing so was to orient myself (as I shall also do for the reader) for preparing questions and absorbing answers from my interviewees within the proper context. I will first discuss patterns of immigration between Latin American and the United States since the 1990s with detailed consideration of the level of impact that the Southeastern region has since experienced. Next, I will briefly focus on globalization and how recent Latino immigration in the South functions as one of its many expressions. I will then proceed to describe the development of the H-2A guestworker visa program: its roots, causes, and effects on the U.S. and Latin America. Descriptions of organizations that have been created in North Carolina as a result of the H-2A program will be used to offer a glimpse at its impact on the social, political, and economic realm. Political policies on a state level will be filtered into the case studies portion of my thesis so that the direct impact that individuals feel can be most truthfully conveyed.

The primary intent of the background section is to provide basic answers to questions concerning farmworkers in North Carolina such as *Why are they here? What purpose do they serve?* and so on. Unfortunately, the domestic resident public is overwhelmingly uninformed of social justice issues concerning farmworkers and the history behind their presence. I hope that briefly exploring the overall circumstances that have attracted Latino immigrants to North Carolina will serve two purposes: first, understanding how each of the case studies highlights the emotional realities, struggles, and experiences of farmworkers; and second, recognizing how their personal narratives contrast with the sterile theory and impersonal data most easily accessible to NC general public. Arreola notes that "the media have largely carried the nationalist banner for Hispanics/Latinos" through newspapers, legislation, and public discourse that readily rely on statistics and labels, cutting the humanistic appeal and connection that could be formed on the basis of shared values and aspirations (2004:34). To counter the naked outlines of "right" versus "illegal," "citizen" versus "alien," that are most often publicized, the hopes and goals revealed through my case studies insist that a uniting force exists within every individual who strives to create a home. Therefore, distinctions between "us" and "them" can be blurred as the reader is challenged to realize that an immigrant is a person, not an "issue."

I interviewed four Latino men who have either participated as an agricultural laborer or offer aid to the farmworker community of North Carolina. I chose to limit my interviewee pool to men because, generally speaking within the agricultural sector, they are the initiators of immigration; I wanted to limit the "pull" factor of North Carolina to exclude pre-existing nuclear family as much as possible. Father Rafa[2], a priest at the Christian Ministry for Farmworkers, was my first interviewee due to our previous relationship based in my participation with an on-campus student group focused on farmworker rights and empowerment. Through Father Rafa, I came into contact with Elias, who also works for CMFF, and, additionally, worked in Southeastern agriculture with his family during his youth. Elias connected me with two undocumented farmworkers, Fito and Arturo, who were

---

[2] Names of all people and organizations involved or revealed through my case studies have been changed for the protection of their identity.

from the same hometown in Mexico as his family. I dedicated individual case studies to Father Rafa, Elias, Arturo, and Fito in order to narrate the human experience of making a home within North Carolina while identifying larger themes, such as family and job opportunity, that significantly influence each story.

My interviews with farmworkers and aid agencies reveal the main challenges of North Carolina that especially effect their formation of "home." Each case study offers a unique perspective on what that person's home is, how they formed it, the oppositions that each has faced in making a home in NC, and how these are, should be, or will be overcome. Through my questions I hoped to understand farmworkers' experience in North Carolina and how their explicit and implicit interactions with culture, politics, economics, and society are expressed through their decision and ability to form a home. The drive to create a home globally unites a spectrum of people; "home is where the heart is," but how, and why, is home?

"Latino" within my research

I use "Latino" within my thesis as an all-encompassing term for populations that originate in Latin America. This includes all states of Mexico, Central America, and South America. I specifically used this term both in negation of the stereotypical "Mexican" term that many use in reference to Latino immigrants within the United States, and with a *regional* rather than a *racial* or *ethnic* mindset. As Ronald Cohen commented in reference to the race/ethnicity divide and overlap, "ethnic group boundaries, rather than being stable and continuous, are 'multiple and overlapping set of ascriptive loyalties that make for multiple identities;'" to deny all immigrants from Latin America the ability to choose their own ethnic loyalty and identity with the assumptive label of "Mexican" is consequentially against the nature and purpose of this thesis (Edmund Hamann 2001:11). Further, it resembles a key challenge to Latino immigrants in finding and creating home that I have observed during my research: silence and neutralization of culture. Rhetoric is a powerful tool, and political campaigns can negatively shape social sentiment towards Latino immigrants; using terms such as "alien," "parasite," and "illegal" in association with "Mexican" strips away regional and personal identity, as well as imposing an insidious cultural "tendency" upon all populations south of our U.S. borders.

Background

Latino Immigration since the 1990s: Statistics

According to the Census Bureau, Latino immigration in North Carolina increased by 50.9% from 1990 to 2000. Further, there was a 273.7% increase of "foreign-born" population between 1990 and 2000 in North Carolina, with almost half (46 %) of the national foreign-born population being of Hispanic origin in 2003. By 2005, the US Census recorded data that detailed the generational status of the US population, since second-generation USA citizens with either one or both parents having been born in a foreign country became a substantial category, 11%, of the 2004 US population.

These statistics invoke a multitude of questions that cannot be answered by mere numbers. North Carolina was the leading state in percentage increase of foreign-born population in 2005; however, what lies underneath this blanketing statistic? The Southeast region, in particular, boasts the top five states (Arkansas, Georgia, South Carolina, Tennessee, and North Carolina) in the growth rate of Hispanic populations between 2000 and 2006. Although the overall Hispanic population does not closely challenge Southwestern states such as Texas, Arizona, or California, the shifting immigrant interest in regional locations cannot be ignored. My goal is to use case studies to flesh out and give a human face to data provided by statistics and censuses. I will explore the appeal of Latino farmworkers to North Carolina specifically, and the USA generically, with enlightening slices of individual perspective concerning movements and interactions that occur beneath the statistical surface of immigration.

Globalization

Globalization can be described as the exposure and intertwining of cultures, countries, societies, and individuals on an international, or global, level that is propelled by the inventions of new communication technologies, international policies, politics, and trade. Although its motive may be most closely tied to corporate or federal investment, its tentacles of effect cross cultural, religious, social, and economic boundaries and affect virtually all levels of community. As cultures intermingle, globalization threatens to "diminish national distinctions" of borders that traditionally maintained separate cultures and ethnicities both

13

geographically and socially (James Cobb and William Stueck 2005:15). Within the U.S., the sudden, unexpected presence of ethnic diversity that accompanied increased international relations of rural and developing areas such as North Carolina, was "both celebrated and denigrated for weaving diverse cultural heritages into national fabric," although the celebration lagged in comparison to immediate discomfort and fear (Susan Bibler Coutin 2003).

Mentioning globalization serves as an educational tool to better understand the shifting roles that a global, rather than national, regional, or local, framework of mind encourages and requires. Margaret Lock remarks that "the United States and Canada are...often held to be without a culture of tradition, except that fostered by ethnic minorities;" although our fledgling history is founded upon immigrant forefathers, our most recent national and international relationships have been based upon consumption and conquest of resources (which include our duty to challenge cultural alignments that detract from our own interests) (2001:44). Whether in terms of "Manifest Destiny" expansion to the west, or "Democratic" aims to civilize Latin American governments and societies, our own migration has paralleled "cultural colonization," that further enforces our dominance (Margaret Lock 2001:44).

The flood of late twentieth and twenty first century immigrants has been met with certain hostility expressed through political and social actions and attitudes. Although the USA has been characterized as a "melting pot" with alternating opposition and acceptance towards flows of European and Asian immigrants, Latino immigrants carry with them an additional, distinguishing, sentiment. Irish and German immigrants were met with equal sneers and accusations of "stealing jobs" as present-day Latinos. However, the root of these historical immigrants' misfortune did not pose the immediate, cyclical, implication of the USA as a source, rather than just a solution, of their troubles as does Latino immigration. Globalization has imposed a consequence for the U.S.' actions and involvement in Latin America that occurs on our own "turf." Further, reactions within the U.S have reflected a mentality of "the best defense is a good offense" through political policies and social slanders that reinforce Lock's idea that "Culture can readily be turned into an 'exclusionary teleology' (Daniel 1991:8), one that mobilizes the notion of an *idealized shared past*, a *reinvented history*" by blanketing the population of Latino immigrants under coordinated labels of

"Mexican," "alien," and "illegal," the effects of which will be elaborated upon within my case studies (Margaret Lock 2001:45). Imposed terminology denies the agency and ownership of one's own culture; "assertions about culture are more often than not simultaneously moral and political claims," and enforce the idea that the Latino immigrant "culture" (since they supposedly only pertain or belong to one) diverts the negative implications of the U.S.' role in inciting this immigration to focus upon the inherent "illegality" of immigrants (Margaret Lock 2001:45).

Let's briefly return to the pre-globalization, national relationship between the South and the rest of the U.S. In terms of regional dominance, the South's potential and worth has suffered slow recognition. Historically, the South lagged behind the northern development of urban and industrial areas, and therefore stalled the accompanying abandonment of dependence in un-free labor that supported its agriculturally based economy. James Peacock notes, "North and South are spacist ways of accentuating opposition, the differences in values, ways of life, histories, and institutions of the two regions of the United States," in reference to the national "role" of the South previous to the impacts of globalization's forces (2007:131). However, within the 21st century, global awareness and interactions create an amplified notion and re-definition of worth: "the old question for the South and for southerners was, 'How do I relate to the nation?' The new question is, 'How do I relate to the world?'" (James Peacock 2007:x). In his anthropological book, *Grounded Globalism,* Peacock suggests that once broadened identifier horizons challenge a traditional role, the required re-orientation and re-assignment of position within a global schematic that succeeds resembles Freud's theory of psycho-historical alignment. Implicitly supporting the notion that "the past repeats itself," the new identity of the South has found its duties in relation to Latin America outlined by its historical relationship of paternalism with the North. The North-South dichotomy has proven resilient on an international level; globalization now allows the South (along with the rest of the nation) to assert a focus and relationship of power upon the new South: Latin America.

The Southern economy has traditionally relied on a basis of cheap imported (agricultural) labor (African slaves began the trend, and with the abolition of slavery, European and Asian immigrants initially filtered in to fill the gaps of labor). With the 21st century bringing global accessibility, blustering and growing cities attracted international

15

investors and economic emphasis (James Cobb and William Stueck 2005:3). However, dependence on imported labor, which is increasingly necessary to support blossoming urban development, continued. This is easily overlooked and forgotten although international laborers lay the foundations (literally-through manual labor, and historically-support of the continued agricultural practices) for the new image of Southern prosperity.

The absence of publically acknowledged *benefits* that immigration and globalization offer the South demonstrates the fear rooted in unbalanced education that not only affects the individual disgruntled citizen, but is also solidified into political policies. Immigration currently carries the label of "threat" in political campaigns, and "the proposed solutions are about restricting, enforcing, deporting, apprehending;" rhetoric that reinforces the precise gap between the socially perceived and actual impacts and origins of immigration (Alejandra Casteñeda 2006:84). Susan Bibler Coutin illustrates how "the emphasis on choice...suggest[s] that the United States simply attract[s] immigrants as a matter of course because of its superior way of life" rather than acknowledging the push/pull factor of globalization, and, in fact, a "nonchoice" of the individual who is controlled by economic, political, and social reactions to smudged national borders and challenged "traditional" identifications (2003:517). Further, it is not hard to enforce condemnation of immigrants' pursuits due to the subtle memory of the USA's own goals for expansion. Whereas Latin American immigrants are seeking refuge from hunger, ideological or political affiliations, and joblessness, these sensations are unfamiliar and therefore widely unacknowledged as the "true" roots and motives for immigration. Rather, our own individualistic goals of self- or nation-motivated gain are easily transferred to the, consequently, demonized Latino immigrant.

State and federal policies struggle to control the force of globalization so that it complies within the boundaries of USA comfort zones. NAFTA, for example, embraced globalization by encouraging the removal of trade barriers between Mexico and the USA (as well as Canada). Conflictingly, it initially expected that although fluidity would replace the restriction of Mexican import tariffs on USA goods, the barrier would retain, and actually increase, its rigidity in terms of human bodies, reflecting how "immigration policies...often failed to achieve their goals because the migration process 'follows a transnational logic,' whereas migration policies 'still follows a national logic'" (Harald Bauder 2006:7). Even as

16

the reality of stimulated, rather than stifled, immigration from Latin America since the 1990s was acknowledged, identities of belonging became more stringent in opposition to those results of globalization.

The social and political challenges that immigrants in North Carolina face presently reflect resistance to the side-effects of globalization that were unexpected and uncontrolled. Blending of identities, *mestizaje*[3], and acceptance of the additional cultural influence to the "Southern Identity" is rejected if it cannot be manipulated to fit within our standards. As Sofia Villenas mentioned in her article concerning Latino immigrants in Appalachian North Carolina, "not only was the human being not welcomed, but also the culture 'difference' they represented was kept in check." (Edmund Hamann 2001:19). The Q'doba, "Tex-Mex," restaurants are a welcome attraction, offering "spicy," "Mexican" food, but it is merely a cardboard representation of any actual culture, and for that reason it poses no threat of change. Migrant laborers fit in nicely to the agricultural structure of the South; however the second-wave development of communities and residence threatened that these individuals are more than labor units, but rather carry with them their own cultural identity. Casteñeda remarks, "if one understands migration as a process of leaving one place and settling down in another, of being pushed out from a region and pulled in by another, then, probably, migrants experience a lack of orientation, a loss of a place they can call home;" however, through a "range of social practices which, taken together, claim and establish a distinct social space," Latino immigrants have created a home on multiple levels (2006:13; Daniel D. Arreola 2004:33).

---

[3] *Mestizaje* is a Spanish term describing the historic category for "mixed blood" offspring in Latin America since its colonization by Spain. *Mestizos* are identified as the resulting population of Spanish "pure-blood" and indigenous coupling. During the 1960s Latin America "Boom" literature movement, *mestizaje* was identified as its goal by writers such as Gabriel García Marquez: to create a single mixed race. It was also proposed as the unique token that Latin America offered to the rest of the world. Historically, *mestizaje*, or the blending of races, that occurs during colonization is due to (generally speaking) imposition of the colonizer's culture (and men) upon that of the indigenous (women). Within the United States, hostility has been a prominent reaction to the surge of Latino immigration from this south and the culture that they carry with them. We fear our own identity as "domestic residents," the 21st century "indigenous" peoples of the USA, its historic connotations, and consequentially "panic in witnessing the metamorphosis of 'home' into a world dominated by sinister aliens" (Carola Suárez-Orozco and Marcelo Suárez-Orozco, 296). Will we be forced to submit our culture to that of the "invaders," "colonizers," as we once did around the world? In the South, do we fear that our resilient tradition will quiver and crumble if we cannot neutralize the threatening, increasing, presence of Latino community and culture?

NAFTA

The North Atlantic Free Trade Agreement (NAFTA) of 1994 is a much-debated, policy that highly impacted (and continues to impact) the relationship between the USA and Mexico and, consequently, immigration between the two countries. My goal in mentioning NAFTA is not to discuss whether it was beneficial or harmful to either country, but merely to briefly explore the connections it may have with immigration trends. NAFTA encouraged privatization, neoliberalism, free-market trade, and capitalism between U.S. and north and south border companions. Mexico, following Canada, had been the second largest consumer of U.S. agricultural exports before the NAFTA trade agreement. However, the competition for Mexico's market during the early nineties (brought on by heightened global awareness and interactions) influenced the U.S.' proposal of NAFTA in order to decrease competition by lowering border tariffs, thereby allowing the continued and increased provision of agricultural goods. The option of cheaper agricultural imports from the U.S. proposed to diminish malnutrition in Mexico. Emphasis was also placed on developing urban areas in Mexico to consequentially create jobs on multiple socio-economic levels and bring Mexico to the forefront of "progress" and international acknowledgement. Even so, "The NAFTA rules of origin for agricultural products were constructed to prevent Mexico from becoming an export platform for processed products made from subsidized raw materials originating in non-NAFTA countries," a position that challenged the "progress" and success of the U.S., rather than Mexico (USDA FAS factsheet 2008).

The subsequent years of the trade agreement witnessed grim instability within the Mexican economy. The immediate devaluation of the peso and stock market crash in Mexico, 1994, posed a stark contrast to the stable stock market and flourishing economy of the United States. NAFTA's immediate impact zone in Mexico was rural agricultural communities, which were unable to compete with the shock of unceasing, cheap, imports from the USA. The proposed solution was that developing urban zones in Mexico would absorb unemployed rural farmers by offering new jobs that dualistically offered social progression. However, the economic consequences of NAFTA proved to be too staggering; urban Mexico could not develop as planned, and, as a result, the unemployed were not greeted within their home country with jobs, and had to shift the direction of their search elsewhere. The impossibility of rural Mexican farms to survive in post-NAFTA environments invoked a "push" factor towards areas that boasted jobs and stability (the treaty had proposed that these areas would be in urban Mexico). Although "agricultural trade has increased in both directions [between Mexico and the USA] under NAFTA from $7.3 billion in 1994 to $20.1 billion in 2006," the benefits are substantially bipolar (USDA FAS fact sheet 2008).

Southeastern Region: Area of Intrigue

Globalization changed the landscape of the South's role on both international and national levels. One the one hand, the agricultural sector discovered staggering price competition from countries that offered cheaper products whose prices directly reflected availability of low-wage labor. In fact, a seasonal migrant visa program sprouted, officially, in the U.S. and Canada as early as the 1980s in order to provide domestic "growers with the labor force necessary to compete with growers in low-wage countries" (Harald Bauder 2006:24). Consequently, "rural areas...suffered the most, accounting for roughly half of the region's job losses since 1979," yet the South was able to prosper from the benefits that globalization offered as well (James Cobb and William Stueck 2005:3). Growing big cities in the Southeast spiked the demand for low-wage labor and easily attracted unemployed populations from Mexico (and Latin America) with its multitude of job opportunities.

The availability of cheap machinery and labor was made possible through the global connections that allowed international investors to extend their services to the South. Attraction was sparked in this region, particularly, due to its "meager wages and lower taxes," in comparison to the rest of the nation, that had historically retarded its regional industrial growth (James Cobb and William Stueck 2005:xii). According to the US Census, the South was the only region to experience a net increase in population due to (domestic) migration from within the U.S. between 2004-2005. The new economic activity of this region, paired with comparatively low costs of living, intrigued audiences within and outside U.S. borders to pursue financial gain. Initially, "job globalization seem[ed] to exacerbate the south's economic unevenness, because it tend[ed] to benefit metropolitan economies while decimating rural ones" until the attractive force of industrial agriculture coupled with the provision of cheap migrant labor provided an alternative to struggling rural communities (James Cobb and William Stueck 2005:3).

Business sectors of the Southeast were "experiencing rapid growth in banking, high-tech sectors and biomedical research that, in turn, expanded the demand for low-wage labor in the service economy and construction industries," which was NAFTA's originally proposed "intent" for Mexican urban areas (James Cobb and William Stueck 2005:3). The stable, or even stimulated, economy that developed and expanded cities in the Southeastern Region additionally provided avenues for "many working-class blacks and whites [to move] up the economic ladder," leaving gaps in the low-wage, labor-intensive, occupational sector that was increasing in demand (Steve Striffler 2007:676). Economic stagnation, and therefore inability to compete on global levels, with which the Southeast historically struggled due to its dependence on agriculture as its primary source of revenue filtered south through the newly tariff-free borders into Mexico.

Latino Migration: The Shift From West to East

Latino migration, distinctively, has had a long history of interactions within the U.S. primarily because of our shared border with Mexico. States such as California, Arizona, and Texas, once Mexican territory, have always had substantial populations of Latino communities and experienced steadily high rates of immigration that result from the combination of recruited agricultural labor and "self-initiated" migration. Western migration traditionally had a two-fold concentration and appeal: the seasonal labor was located relatively near to the country of origin and any family that still lived there, and the sustained existence of Latino communities within principally urban areas (e.g. Los Angeles).

Western social justice movements (primarily in California) of the 60's and 70's focused on a new population of "chicanos," which were self-defined as second-generation Mexican offspring born in the USA. One tier of these movements emphasized educational opportunity and fighting the inherent racism of secondary school systems that discouraged Chicano students from applying to and attending college. Multiple-generation investment of Mexican and Latino-origin communities within the western U.S. is expressed through this social justice movement. The fact that equal access to higher education and achievement began as early as 45 years ago also testifies to the existence, if not incorporation, of Latino populations within Western culture and recent history. Community strength is provided by the populations' political presence as citizens that can vote and therefore demand that their voice, protests, and suggestions be heard. Southeastern Latinos have yet to establish a firm first, let alone politically recognized second, generation.

However, "the presence of long-standing Latino communities with well-established practices for incorporating new arrivals" that originally pulled migration towards the West eventually became a challenge to new-wave migrants (Steve Striffler 2007:676). Chicanos of the West have built an identity that distinguishes them from new immigrants on the basis of status as citizens and the history of their struggle to establish themselves within western culture. New immigrants threaten to tarnish that identity, and are often made into scapegoats for the "negative" impacts that domestic residents attribute to Latinos such as increased crime, for example. Therefore, the schism of identities, paired with the overpopulation of historic Latino communities and correspondingly high competition for jobs, pushed un-established immigrants towards new destinations.

Steve Striffler proposes that the original appeal of Southeastern U.S. was that "'the family' became possible in a way it had never been in California (or even Mexico)," due to abundant low-competition jobs and relatively low Hispanic population (in the early 1990s) that allowed new immigrants and accompanying family members to create their own communities (2007:674). Therefore immigration to the Southeast in part reflects hope for individuals to work, "seeking to realize [their] greatest potential and to fulfill [them]selves" without having to be deprived of time with their family or a home (Brett Williams 1991:65). Permanent jobs are offered in poultry plants and construction sites but not agriculture. Pursuit of agriculture-specific jobs is accepting an inherent seasonal limit to the time spent within any particular region. As a grower, there is more flexibility and possibility of sedentary settlement; however, money is required to purchase or rent land, consequentially requiring multiple years of investment and savings. A farmworker lifestyle is not optimal for creating a family immediately. Many Latino immigrants choose to become an agricultural laborer because it provides financial stability and employment, which is not as widely available in their country of origin. Additionally, this job offers the opportunity to learn agricultural techniques that pertain to the Southeast; paired with the possibility of forming connections and saving up money to invest in land, a farmworker may eventually become a grower, as was the case of Elias' father. This notion reflects the migrant farmworkers' consideration of "home" as an aspiration for the future, their years of seasonal labor merely laying down foundations for an eventual home and family.

H-2A Program: Past and Present

The H-2A temporary working visa program provides growers in the U.S. the opportunity to recruit specific numbers of legal international laborers to work on their farms during the growing season. Certain requirements are expected of the workers and growers in accordance with the H-2 policy (there is also an H-2B program for non-agricultural seasonal workers in the U.S.). Before applying to the program, growers must first become certified by the United States Department of Labor (DOL) and the United States Citizenship and Immigration Service (USCIS). To receive certification, the grower is required to prove that effort has been exerted towards recruiting laborers within the U.S. but that there were not a sufficient number of domestic laborers available to work in their fields. The grower is then allowed to request a specific number of laborers about 90 days before they anticipate the beginning of the harvest season.

The certification standards reveal a complex, largely misunderstood and/or ignored, entanglement between U.S. growers, federal policy, public knowledge, and international immigrants. Requirements concerning domestic laborers implicate a significant gap in the domestic agricultural workforce; additionally, during the first half of the harvest season, growers must hire any and all domestic laborers if they are "ready, willing, and able to perform the job" (US DOL factsheet). Either there are too few available domestic citizens to contribute to agricultural labor, or too few *willing* workers within the U.S. What would they not be willing to do? Work on a seasonal basis with additional requirements of extended working days in order to collect the harvest in sufficient time, perhaps. Unlike H-2A laborers, domestic employees would benefit from the income taxes (with at least social security) that are weeded from immigrant paychecks, though as "guestworkers," immigrant laborers do not receive these benefits. However, the H-2A program continues to appeal to more immigrants than there are positions even though they are excluded from some of the benefits that a domestic laborer would receive.

Unlike the majority of jobs in U.S. present society, agricultural work maintains certain restrictions despite "advancements" in farming technology and machinery.

Additionally, the NC Department of Labor (DOL) identifies the major agricultural products of North Carolina (blueberries, strawberries, melons, tomatoes, and tobacco) as "hand harvested and labor intensive," therefore retaining a certain pre-industrialism quality. Compromising in terms of daily (or weekly) working hours is not as easily accessible during the harvest season, when the produce must be collected, in comparison with other white and blue-collar jobs. Even so, it remains a rudimentary component of our society: it provides us food! Even if U.S. citizens have evolved or progressed past this sort of employment, someone must fill these gaps, and international immigrants willingly do so. Presently, 90% of U.S. farmworkers are Hispanic (James Cobb and William Stueck 2005:78).

The H-2A program evolved from the Bracero program, which was established to support U.S. growers during World War II. The wartime societal skew dramatically impacted the availability of able-bodied laborers to work in the fields during the harvest and sustain economic production on the agricultural front. Further, industrial production of war machines and supplies within factories became a new distraction that further pulled remaining workers towards urban zone. In 1942, the federal government enacted the Bracero program that legally recruited Mexican workers to fill the labor abyss under which growers suffered and to ensure that domestic production of food continued. This program dwindled to an end in 1964 due to a medley of dysfunctions.

Firstly, as WWII U.S. soldiers returned, the additional presence of the recruited workers created sudden job competition that resulted in downward spiraling wages and worker rights. This spiked hostility and division between domestic residents of rural agricultural towns and the braceros who had ensured the survival of these farming towns during soldiers' absences. Secondly, the Bracero program's immigrant policies did not incorporate federal regulations, but rather constituted individual contracts between the workers and each private grower. Problems concerning human and worker rights violations were a direct result of geographic isolation that shattered the possibility of a united "voice" to protest, residential antagonism, and linguistic and cultural barriers. The general public's heightened awareness and protest of the mistreatment of farmworkers within the Bracero program encouraged its demise. During the congressional creation of the H-2 program, new regulations were highlighted to dissuade such problems from reoccurring.

North Carolina Growers Association (NCGA) and H-2A in NC

Presently, 45,000 seasonal guest workers are provided temporary visas per year through the H-2A program. North Carolina has led the country in H-2A program participation by annually recruiting 10,000 workers (NCGA website). Each year, North Carolina growers are responsible for submitting to the North Carolina Growers Association (NCGA) the number of workers they need for the upcoming season. They are expected to support their hired workers with minimum wages (set annually by the Federal Government that determines the "average regional wage earned by farmworkers"), housing that meets Occupational Safety and Health Administration (OSHA) standards[4], workers compensation insurance (at least ¾ of the wages stated in the contract; these are negotiable because of the volatile nature of agricultural profits based on the success of the harvest), and transportation to and from to their country of origin at the beginning and end of the contract.

The NCGA is the largest recruitment agency for H-2A visa holders in the nation. The website advertises advantages that it offers to growers by "deal[ing] with the beaurocrats so that you can concentrate on what you do best- farming!" Farmers are offered a legal, "reliable," easy way to receive the labor that they need in the fields. The NCGA boasts of a staff of "Spanish speakers who assist you in resolving any communication issues that arise while your workers are here," and functions as the middleman between growers, politicians, and H-2A employees. Their role allows a disconnection between growers and their recruited farmworkers; no face-to-face interviews are necessary, the language barrier is maintained, and migrant workers are offered to growers as "labor units" that growers must apply for, rather than people. The NCGA advertisements subliminally deem communication between employers and employees as unnecessary. These observations are not intended to attack growers, or imply that all growers view workers as objects; instead, they merely allow a glimpse at networks that make this level of separation and dehumanization possible.

---

[4] 24 states within the USA have "OSHA-approved state plans" for agricultural operations that further specify the standards that each state requires. North Carolina is one of these states, and regulations for housing/living conditions are therefore outlined, inspected, and enforced by the NCDOL. A 1997 North Carolina State University graduate student project had students and farmworkers working together to discuss improvements that were most desired for housing conditions. The following were the answers listed on the NCDOL website:
- Working bathrooms
- Roofs having no leaks
- Homes meeting codes
- Regulations that were enforced
- Homes that were decent
- A wish that "the home was mine"

Several aid agencies have confronted the NCGA for the manner in which they have handled H-2A workers within the U.S. In 2004, a lawsuit was charged against the NCGA for "blacklisting" H-2A workers by coercing them to return home early, thereby breaking the H-2A contract, and consequently making them ineligible to return to the program. Laborers that attempted to raise awareness of mistreatment on the fields (no water being available during the day, inability to seek medical treatment for injuries, etc.) were those on whom the NCGA focused their efforts to send home. This lawsuit was carried out by North Carolina Justice Department, one of the many organizations that have supported farmworkers and have attempted to lessen their vulnerability as employees in North Carolina. FLOC (Farm Labor Organizing Committee) is another aid agency that focuses on unionizing workers to break through the geographical and social isolation that renders them voiceless and easily manipulated or abused. FLOC strives to empower H-2A workers by encouraging them to participate politically, voice their concerns and fight to improve their working and living conditions, and by 2007 a "collective bargaining agreement" was reached between FLOC and NCGA on behalf of H-2A workers. However, some conflict has emerged regarding undocumented farmworkers, whose presence may be a challenge to H-2A workers' legitimacy and rights within North Carolina as documented employees. Through my case studies, I explore the conditions such as isolation, voicelessness, inhuman living and working conditions, and being perceiving as a "problem" rather than a "person," that documented and undocumented farmworkers must endure, as well as the effect they have on farmworkers' ability to attain "home." CMFF is one of many aid agencies in North Carolina that hope to offer a welcoming "at home" environment to farmworkers during their employment.

Case Studies

Purpose

The three case studies within my thesis unfold the perspectives of four individuals who have migrated to and resided in North Carolina for at least the past six years. Their motives for coming and staying in North Carolina, as well as the challenges through which they have suffered and fought, are distinct. Although the H-2A visa is a national program, globalization is an international phenomenon, and "in this so-called global era, people still seek and find a place to call home" (James Peacock 2007:10). I have found that there is not one solution, goal, or consequence, not a single answer to my question of "what is home" to a farmworker in North Carolina. In spite of the idea that everyone *understands* the "abiding desire for home," it is unquestionably personal (James Peacock 2007:10). The struggles, challenges, and cultural environment that every person experiences create distinctly tweaked definitions and significances of home. These case studies explore "only diverse peoples struggling to remain who they are while becoming someone else" through influences by social, economic, and political sectors as they pursue home (Daniel Arreola 2004:33).

I will present the case studies in the same sequential order that I had the interviews so that my own personal process of growing to understand the different components and creations of home will develop at the same pace and in the same order. Each interview was affected by new ideas that were offered or expanded by the former. I found many similarities, and a plethora of contradictions, between each individual perspective of reality. Along with the value that each case study offers independently, weaving the exposed root values and experiences together into a group philosophy will better reflect how a home and community may be constructed.

Three Variations of "Home"

I have identified three categories of home sentiment that farmworkers in North Carolina identify with, none of which are mutually exclusive. Interview responses from farmworkers and aid agency representatives conveyed emphases that balanced between a focus on the past, present, and future as well as economic and social investment in their definition of home[5]. Overall, I have perceived home to be contingent on three variations of how an individual's life is oriented around time, and how this effects the investment of their accomplishments. Creating different constructs of home, I have found that within the North Carolina farmworker community, actions and decisions are based upon which theoretic "home" they pursue and incorporate into their own aspirations.

The first way that a farmworker may consider "home," is as an ideal that he hopes and works towards for the future of his family (whether or not it exists at the time he initiated migration). Focus upon an ideal family home may have begun while the farmworker was

---

[5] Full transcripts of the interviews that I held are available in the appendix section.

still in his country of origin; contrarily, the ideal equally could have not been fully materialized until immigrants came to the U.S. Documentation does not affect this sentiment of home held by farmworkers, and it is equally applicable to farmworkers that uphold this ideal by channeling investment to their country of origin and those who dedicate their pursuits to North Carolina. The consistent, core, concept is the dedication of the present to build up a future. Correspondingly, the farmworker's family may already exist in their country of origin prior to immigration or it could be created within North Carolina (the "family" that I refer to is nuclear family, the elements of which will be discussed more in depth in a specific section of Father Rafa's case study). Families created in the US are generally considered the most threatening option by domestic residents. Hannah Gill addresses the reality behind residents' perceived threat by describing how "demographic changes are due to births more than immigration, illustrating how Latin Americans are building communities and families in North Carolina," (2006:29).

The second "home" sentiment possibly held by a farmworker is an idyllic image of the past that is internally carried to North Carolina within his heart. When I imagine this "home," I think of the e.e. cummings poem *"i carry your heart with me (i carry it in my heart)."* Although this poem is written in reference to a lover, I believe that the concept can be applied to carrying one's "home" with them as well. In maintaining North Carolina as an area for business and economic advancement, solely, a farmworker is able to distance himself from the reality of his situation (poor living conditions, separation from family, meager wages, etc.), and concentrate on his cherished and protected home of his heart. This home is the idealized past, memories of family and belonging that a farmworker uses to endure his present situation. Even though the work he does is invested in the home of his past, there is a clear separation between that cherished memory and the life that he lives in order to protect and maintain it. H-2A workers are able to keep their children and family separate from the realities of their job due to the physical distance; however, often times the unintended sacrifice is that a farmworker's home continues to change and grow during absence as well. Resulting sentiments of home as "beautiful and unbearable at the same time" emerge to symbolize the ideal towards which the farmworker strives yet may never be able to accomplish due to necessary cyclical absence (Steve Striffler 2007:680). Contact with family in countries of origin strengthens the image of home as well as the resolve to continue struggling within North Carolina in order to maintain it; H-2A workers who are able to return at the end of every season are most likely to identify with this home concept.

The work of CMFF and other aid agencies in North Carolina places importance on the two previously mentioned concepts of home. They provide calling cards and other methods to facilitate communication and contact between a farmworker and his family, as well as providing childcare for fledgling families. Therefore, aid agencies administer certain dedication towards cultivating the achievement of both these "home" sentiments. Simultaneously, great effort is exerted in creating and providing a slice of home, family, and community with their struggle to ameliorate working and living conditions in North Carolina. Again, promoting feelings of welcome, care, and empowerment are not identical to encouraging permanent settlement. Programs are formed in *support* of farmworkers who come to North Carolina to labor for the benefit of the United States, because they deserve recognition as persons. People, humans, crave a "home away from home;" a tolerable, sustainable, livable environment is the third home-like sentiment that programs of empowerment, communities of support, and ministries hope to provide.

Case Study #1: Father Rafa

Introduction

I met Father Rafa during the summer of 2008 when I organized a student trip to visit farmworkers camps. Father Rafa is the priest for Christian Ministry for Farmworkers (CMFF), an aid organization in central North Carolina that began in 1982. He came to the United States specifically to work with CMFF in 1996, two years before a permanent facility was constructed, and close to the initiation of the annual Farmworker Fair.

I had hoped that many students would be able to travel to CMFF with me that summer; we were going to discuss our involvement with the September Farmworker, an end-of-season appreciation and send-off for all farmworkers, families, and communities (not just Latino) that interacted with or surrounded the Ministry. Although I was only able to bring three additional students, Father Rafa was welcoming and enthusiastic about our commitment to the Farmworker Fair, as well as our potential to outreach to other university students in

Chapel Hill. Father Rafa exudes warmth, provokes laughter that includes everyone, and holds the perfect balance of respecting and being respected by those he interacts with. We kept in contact over time, and he was the first person that I contacted to interview.

CMFF is located in rural eastern North Carolina, its primary motive being to nestle itself in the midst of the highest-farmworker-density area. The facility, itself, is a simple one-story building surrounded by flat fields that, during the Farmworker Fair, were used as soccer fields and parking lots. Inside, the waiting lounge of CMFF has strategically-placed bulletin boards with informational brochures concerning legal aid, health agencies, child-care services, and "Know Your Rights" sheets. Lining the office walls where I interviewed Father Rafa were poster-sized photos that had been taken by a Newsweek photographer, and revealed the stark living conditions of farmworker camps. The largest room inside the facility is bare with many windows and a couple of cabinets and fold-out chairs; this room is used for Father Rafa's Sunday services if lousy weather constrains them from the preferred, more accommodating to large congregations, outdoors. Father Rafa described recent harvest seasons when entire busloads of farmworkers traveled from camps to CMFF specifically for the Sunday services. His joy and satisfaction at the accomplishment of the program radiated as he told me of the farmworkers that had confessed to him, "to come here every Sunday is to come to a party; we feel very happy."

Although it also provides several programs of its own, CMFF focuses mostly on multidimensional outreach and providing of information. Meaning that they are a nucleus, extending themselves to students, religious groups, community members, and farmworkers to both offer and receive service. Family is central to Father Rafa's work at CMFF, whether it is ensuring that farmworkers can maintain contact with family in their country of origin, supporting newly-formed families of North Carolina, or hoping to create a family through the Farmworker Fair, church services, and by covering basic social and natural needs. Though CMFF offers their programs to all individuals, regardless of documentation status, they perceive H-2A workers to have the most need, in the highest risk of being exploited, and therefore work closely with their camps. CMFF thus addresses all three sentiments of home though they channel specific energy through programs such as the Farmworker Fair to making a "home away from home" for farmworkers in North Carolina. Concerning home, Father Rafa's mission is to ensure that "when the farmworkers come, they understand that the CMFF is part of their home. Because when they come in they are accepted, they are very welcome, and they feel like a family, like a home. They feel here that they have some of [their] home."

Why Farmworkers are Here

Father Rafa was explicit in explaining that the agricultural sector of North Carolina attracts immigrants whose previous lives were not necessarily spent being a farmworker. A compelling quality to many is the previously discussed availability of low-wage, low-competition, jobs that the Southeastern region has been able to boast of since the mid 1990's. Further, the lower cost of living (comparatively to the rest of the nation) of this region poses greater potential for workers outside of the H-2A program to be able to afford housing, and eventually establish a life and family. All considering, North Carolina poses an attractive alternative to the slackened economic situation of many Latin American countries from which migrant workers originate. Whether hearing from family, members of the community, or through billboard advertisements, the promise of available work provides a constant flow of migrants to North Carolina whose "destinations [are often times] already determined through home-village networks" (James Cobb and William Stueck 2005:82).

Following their decision to participate in the H-2A program, some migrants, according to Father Rafa "cannot [support] the work at the camp because it is too hard," whereas others "say, 'no, I love the camp. I love the agriculture.'" The 2001-2002 NWAS survey uncovered that 72% of farmworkers expected that their future, for at least the next five years, would involve a continuation of agricultural work (2005). The proposed idea that, within the farmworker population of North Carolina, some choose their occupation out of love for agriculture, working with one's hands, with the land, is estranged from a large part of North Carolina present-day society. The social identity of the Southeastern region has, generally, deviated away from its historical roots of an agriculturally based lifestyle. Therefore, it is increasingly difficult for a domestic resident to understand that some farmworkers pursue "these opportunities [that] are offered to them in Mexico" because agriculture is a part of their identity (Father Rafa). As discussed in the NAFTA section, the continuous flood of cheap produce from the U.S. decimated rural areas in Mexico; the US increased corn exports to Mexico by 240% while also eliminating corn subsidies so that the ability compete with U.S. imports and support a family with traditional farming was close to impossible (USDA). As a result, over 2 million Mexicans have been forced to end their employment and lifestyles as farmers since the introduction of NAFTA in 1994 (SAF fact sheet). Individuals who hope to sustain their agricultural existence find an avenue towards doing so in the U.S. by becoming laborers in the fields, and begin the process of owning and working with land from the bottom up. Agricultural labor is no longer a job that many domestic residents can identify with, nor is it considered a stable way to support a family; yet Father Rafa asserts that farmworkers "come here [to North Carolina] because there is the agriculture…is the most important in this state." As a result, North Carolina poses an opportunity for immigrants to continue in the occupation with which they feel the deepest connection.

Immigrants who come to North Carolina as farmworkers, yet have never previously depended on manual labor to support themselves economically, also contradict with commonly held belief that Latino immigrants are lured by the better conditions of the U.S. In describing this second group of farmworkers, Father Rafa states, "there are many people that are not familiar with fields. Some of them are electricians, some of them are mechanics, some…work in computers, some are technicians. They can not work in their countries because there is no job for them." Their choice to participate in agricultural work in North Carolina demands that these individuals also set aside their past dedication, education, and experience. Does this comply with the stereotype that the U.S. promises immigrants a better life, or rather, is it merely the best possible alternative to the unemployment threats within their country of origin?

How prevalent is the threat of unemployment within North Carolina society? Currently, it has become more potent due to our own "economic crisis," yet Mexico has struggled with a stagnant and struggling economy for at least ten years. A participant of the Organization of Economic Cooperation and Development (OECD), a database containing economic-detailed statistics of 30 nations since 1961, Mexico's "registered unemployment rates" have not been included since 2004 due to "standardization conflicts" (OECD website). Employment within Mexico included at least an hour of (monetarily) compensated work within the prior week, although OECD primarily runs on a monthly time-line; hence, the conflicting data. Within Mexico, the informal market of street vendors, mechanics, fruit vendors, etc. is abundant and categorized as employment. Because the state does not offer a support net of unemployment benefits, as do countries such as the U.S. and Canada, unemployment within Mexico implicates a "privilege," and therefore comparison of statistics to countries that offer aid are often skewed (Jonathan Clark: 2005).

INEGI, the Mexican government's organization for statistical and geographic information, reported in 2005 that more than 28% of Mexican citizens were employed through the informal economy, a phenomenon that is decidedly less prevalent within North Carolina society (Jonathan Clark: 2005). Further, over 50% of the unemployed in Mexico have completed their secondary education (UniversiaKnowledge@Wharton, 2005). This statistic indicates the unavailability of a future that many families within Mexico struggle with. Even with the funds to provide education, a study done by Olga Bustos of the National Autonomous University of Mexico, Mexico City, warns that over the span of "six years, 813,169 young graduates will be unable to find jobs, despite their degrees in medicine, dentistry, law, accounting, business administration, architecture, civil engineering, and communications" (Jonathan Clark: 2005). As a result, statistics that portray low unemployment rates in Mexico are, in fact, conveying "the need for persons to subsist through any work at all, rather than a situation of full employment;" the plausibility of unemployment looms at all levels of society, whether or not a university or highschool degree has been achieved, a phenomenon that is unrecognizable to North Carolina residents who depend on higher education as the preliminary step to success, or at least stability (Susan Fleck and Constance Sorrentino 1994: 3).

The underlying theme of this economics and unemployment discussion is to show how Mexican citizens, whom compose 75% of the U.S. farmworker population, have found it necessary to seek employment through formal and informal avenues to survive (SAF fact sheet). Traveling to the U.S., regardless of past experience, education, or occupational alignment, through H-2A or without documentation, is merely a globalized expression of these individuals seeking stability, firmer foundations for their home, and a brighter, more attainable future for their family. Father Rafa contends that the goal of immigrant farmworkers is to support their families, a recognizable feat, yet the manners in which they pursue this goal is unfamiliar and therefore threatening to domestic North Carolinians; he believes that to "show the realities of the [farmworker] camp," is the first step towards acceptance and understanding.

Challenges to Home

> FATHER RAFA: "When I came here…12 years ago, and I visit[ed] the camps where the farmworkers live, I spent more than two years without resting well because, especially during the night, I was trying to, to, to sleep, and I was thinking how [can] these people live in these camps? In these unhuman, unhuman conditions because they don't have any. They don't have shoes, they don't have underwear, they don't have a bed, they don't have chairs, they don't have a kitchen…they don't have any, any, any, and they don't have family"

Father Rafa, before coming to work at CMFF, had congregations of farmworkers in the mountains of Columbia for whom he provided service, yet he is still haunted by the conditions in which farmworkers of North Carolina must live and work. This, in itself, challenges the naive assumption of domestic residents that "anything is better than where they come from." The efforts of Father Rafa and CMFF are to expel these misconceptions through educational outreach and consequential interactions between farmworker and non-farmworker communities, to incite conversation and battle inequality through publicity and awareness. CMFF targets factors that challenge farmworkers' ability to create a home in North Carolina. This does not mean that their aim is to encourage immigrants to settle permanently, but rather to promote "love, respect, justice, peace, help, support" so that while they are in North Carolina, "they can live like human beings" (Father Rafa interview).

Substandard living conditions of farmworkers were a prevalent theme in Father Rafa's discourse. He gave specific notice to the enforcement of laws, both in echoing many domestic residents' concern for undocumented immigration, as well as housing and health codes. Rather than placing blame on immigrants for coming to the United States in pursuit of work, Father Rafa holds culpable, "the same government that let accommodate in jobs, in institutions, 12 million or 13 millions of people" by slackening regulations and penalties for offering employment to workers without documentation. The 1986 Immigration Reform and Control Act (IRCA) provided a process for undocumented workers within the U.S. to apply for residency with the included promise that employers would be held to higher standards, with stricter sanctions, for hiring undocumented individuals. However, the practice of hiring undocumented workers remains prevalent, including within North Carolina agriculture. Father Rafa's favored solution is to grant amnesty for farmworkers and undocumented workers whose contributions and investment to the US are undeniable. Being already "installed" within North Carolina, amnesty would allow these populations to also contribute through income taxes, which are a highlighted concern among domestic residents in response to undocumented immigration, and receive social security benefits since at least thirty percent of farmworkers have family incomes that place them below poverty guidelines (NAWS 2005). Concurrently, Father Rafa depends on the U.S. government to hold employers to a higher accountability in hiring undocumented immigration, since this practice results in fissures not only between domestic and immigrant populations, but within the Hispanic population as well (details will be provided in Elias' section). However, he laments that in reality, "this government won't do any[thing] for the farmworkers" due to the isolation of the farmworker community from those who can "make noise" about the injustice of their position and offer productive solutions.

Accessibility of justice for farmworkers is challenged at multiple levels. Susan Bibler Coutin notes that "migrants are desired as laborers but are excluded from certain public benefits, praised for contributing to society but suspected of maintaining disparate loyalties," for which they are overwhelmingly punished (2003). The work of migrant farmworkers in our agricultural fields is what ensures us oranges and avocados at cheap prices (or even at all) throughout the entire year, yet we are disconnected from the person that provides us this service. The slogan for National Farmworker Awareness Week touts, "Got Food? Thank a Farmworker!" which reinforces the idea that *awareness* of farmworkers should coincide with *appreciation* for the service they provide us through adverse conditions, rather than scorn based upon their origins. Father Rafa stresses, "God gives to each one a gift. And thanks to the gift we can live because if we won't have farmworkers we will die because we won't have any to eat. And for the reason they are farmworkers;" however, society teaches us to consider this "gift" as an assumed privilege if not *our* gift to *them* by providing jobs and "opportunity" (alongside resentment and distrust, of course).

Assumed understanding of farmworkers as (threatening, presumably illegal) "immigrants" rather than "people" within domestic resident populations of nearby communities is what Father Rafa credits as responsible for the existence of subhuman conditions without protest. He explains the irony of our concern for international terrorism, while within our backyards, pesticides are poisoning the producers of our food: "we make noise, we talk about the, the lethal weapons and something like this. And we have here, in our country, in our fields, lethal weapons." Rather than merely blaming outlier communities, he instills the importance of education and awareness, saying, "to reach them, they must know what is happening in our camps" so that safety, if not justice, is provided.

This worry transcends to a theoretical level concerning globalization in which "the shift of focus from civil rights to human rights could work to enhance both concerns by grounding civil rights in the wider human issue, or it could divert attention from pressing local injustices in favor of global concerns" (James Peacock 2007:200). Global awareness cripples our ability to look locally at violation of rights, and therefore challenges the farmworkers' ability to feel welcomed, at home, while he performs a necessary function within our society. Lawsuits concerning pregnant farmworkers who, while picking tomatoes doused in pesticides, were infected and injured the development of their child, 7 cases of modern-day slavery in Florida (to date since 1997), deaths due to simple dehydration are happening within our Southeastern region, yet their geographic proximity is trumped by global concerns for civil war in Darfur, freedom in Tibet, and human rights violations in Afghanistan (for example). How are we able to send money, thoughts, prayers, and organize campaigns for victims across oceans while we eat a BLT (bacon, lettuce, tomato) sandwich that testaments to equal injustices that are concurrently taking place no more than an hour outside of our door? Are we less scared to demand change of perpetuators who we will never see (except through the TV) than of our systems, our stereotypes, and ourselves?

The H2-A Farmworker and his Family

> KOEHLER: When someone says home, the word, is there a specific image or emotion or smell or anything else that comes to mind?
> FATHER RAFA: "When we talk about a home we have, initially we have a place but...we can not...understand...a home without a family living inside of this place"

I began each of my interviews with the question: "how do you define home?" Immediately, Father Rafa replied, "Okay, my definition of a home is a family." He expanded his thoughts by saying that "home" does include a certain location, but, to him, the key component is the existence of family. Perhaps, then, it is because of his personal regard for the importance of family that he also believed that for farmworkers, "to be in touch with their families is the most important" while they are employed in North Carolina. Family is emphasized by Father Rafa as a primary focus for farmworkers that can also invoke an emotional connection with other populations and communities. This bond is often neutralized and rejected through political discourse concerning the "immigration problem."

H-2A workers are employed on a temporary visa that lasts the duration of the harvest season (March-October in North Carolina) and required to complete this contract, without returning home or leaving early, in order to be eligible for the subsequent years' programs. As a result, a schism between time and money investment develops within a farmworkers' contextual lifestyle. The H-2A laborer invests the majority of the year apart from family, whereas the received financial outcomes are devoted to supporting family and building up community within the country of origin (even though benefits of labor: food availability, trade profits, etc. are not received by this country either). Father Rafa described a personal account of the turmoil this can wreak on an individual's life:

Some farmworkers...say to me, they show me the pictures of their houses. Pretty houses. And they say "we could make this thanks to this work because we save money and we use this money to have better homes," and, and they say "I have better homes but I have in my heart vacuums because I couldn't share with my children, my wife, and I lost the best time."

The sacrifice of a father for his family, of parents in order to provide "a better life" for their children is not a foreign concept within the United States. H-2A workers choose to address financial woes and support their family with their agricultural labor in the U.S. Emotional distress derived from the inability to be with one's family is intensified by the indifferent if not hostile social attitudes that "greet" farmworkers in North Carolina. Not only are they unwelcome despite their contribution to the U.S., but also, "as a consequence of immigration laws undocumented migrants get physically separated from the rest of the population by a continual informal judgment that pushes people to accept any kind of job situation" and indecent living and working conditions to continue without being challenged (Alejandra Casteñeda 2006:90). Father Rafa elaborates,

I have seen some videos from Africa, and, that, I know that in Africa there are special places where the people suffer suffer suffer, very much but I saw some videos from Africa and I could conclude that people in Africa live in better conditions than the migrants. You can see. The migrants, the, the number one for the migrant is his family. His family

H-2A workers attempt to maintain family solidarity to extreme lengths. Father Rafa described how many camps do not have public phones, so that on their free day (usually Sundays), workers will walk up to an hour to the nearest town to call their family. Growers are required to provide transportation to their employees between the fields and their residence, but not to outside communities. As a result, travel to buy groceries, call families, go to church services, and so on, is treated as a privilege rather than a right to farmworkers. The burden of spending up to eight months of the year away from one's family carries heavy consequences that are difficult to escape; one H-2A visa holder confided in Father Rafa, saying, "I came to North Carolina trying to have better life and [that] was not what it was. Destruction."

Despite the negativity of being separated from one's families, the H-2A program continues and grows annually in North Carolina. Father Rafa explains, "the worst for any people, any man, and woman, is to be separated from their families, of course;" however, this sacrifice is one that many workers agree to undertake. There seems to be, for many, a mentality that North Carolina agricultural is a means to a happier end; as a consequence, will North Carolina ever carry a home-like sentiment for them? If farmworkers depend on the snippets of conversation with family that occur only weekly, are they truly coming to North Carolina to live or to *endure* until they *can* live?

Manners of dually achieving the ability to work and to be with one's family, participate in one's home, vary. Some farmworkers leave the H-2A program either to return to their country of origin or to reside permanently in the United States. Father Rafa, understanding the importance of home, strives to offer temporary solutions through CMFF services. Alejandra Casteñeda notes that "while migrants recognize that they left home because it was economically insecure- because home excluded their own imagined futures- the experience of displacement makes migrants narrate an idyllic 'place called home,' a place where they belong and where they feel themselves to be a part, as citizens;" Father Rafa holds a double focus of assisting farmworkers' efforts to maintain contact with their families as well as providing "a piece of home" in creating CMFF family and community environments (2006:14; Father Rafa interview). His services, therefore, promote ease in transition (either a continuous balance or a permanent shift) between the second concept of home, farmworkers' families abroad, and the third concept of "idyllic" belonging and home in North Carolina.

CMFF Service
> FATHER RAFA: "I feel really happy when I get home. I have my wife, my children visit me once in a while, but every minute of our life is trying to live the love…Every minute of our life we try to do the best loving and respecting and helping and trying to do the best for others."

When I asked Father Rafa about the goal for farmworkers who came to North Carolina, he responded, "a place where they can live like human beings" is what they seek. The CMFF provides a myriad of programs, as well as information of programs that other agencies offer, in order to assist farmworkers in achieving that goal. Today, Father Rafa estimates that up to 8,000 farmworkers are reached through the programs that CMFF provides. Whether it is childcare services, legal, educational, religious, basic or social needs, CMFF and Father Rafa offer a holistic package to best accommodate farmworkers while they are working in the NC and help them feel welcomed.

At the beginning of Father Rafa's career in North Carolina, he struggled with his outreach to farmworkers because of the church denomination with which he is affiliated. The most prevalent religious denomination of Latin America is the Roman Catholic Church. Father Rafa was originally ordained through this church; however, upon meeting and falling in love with his wife, he decided to shift affiliations and dedicate himself to a denomination that would allow him to marry. Although the first years of the CMFF weekly Sunday services contained congregations of less than twenty members, the determination of Father Rafa to care for farmworkers in camps surrounding the facility eventually overcame their original wariness of his unknown church. The ministry extends the love and care of a family to farmworkers through programs that break down the social and geographical barrier that surrounds them.

The isolation of a farmworker is dangerous yet also implicit within the agricultural, rural, lifestyle. Farms will not be located on the side of interstate highways, alongside bustling cities, or within reach of a local community center. However, the geographic isolation that accompanies agricultural work can be, and has been, somewhat heightened to allow for certain manipulation and an asserted disconnect to occur both within guestworker (H-2A) and undocumented worker camps.

Growers employ H-2A workers individually, who are therefore usually unable to choose the camps where they live or the people that they live with. Undocumented workers, on the other hand, may travel individually or join/create a work crew with people from their hometown, so that they at least know the people that they live and work with. In both scenarios, segmentation between labor camps ensures a fragmented "population," and representation, of farmworkers, and challenges the creation of community solidarity outside the confinements of each individual camp. Further, language barriers heighten the distance between farmworkers and surrounding communities of domestic residents, as well as minimal transportation resources and free time. CMFF has dedicated years towards combating the barriers that confine farmworkers to "live separate, isolated...like perfect slaves," by weaving a network within the farmworkers, themselves, as well as between farmworkers and outside communities (Father Rafa interview).

An important component of CMFF outreach is incorporating outlier communities of domestic residents and working to create opportunities for direct interaction with farmworkers that encourage a more intimate relationship than merely producer/consumer. A process of mutual education is encouraged through programs that the ministry offers such as English as a Second Language (ESL), food and clothing distribution, and their annual Farmworker Fair. ESL classes provide farmworkers and their family access to the language that gives them substance and power within the US, as well subliminally growing to realize that members of English-speaking communities, as well, support and care for them as individuals.

Members of churches, student or community organizations, and otherwise unaffiliated individuals who may not have knowledge of the life and circumstances of farmworkers, are included in CMFF outreach through clothing and food distribution options and the Fair. Father Rafa emphasizes education and outreach towards "the churches, the government, by friendship, by something. To help, reach these people, and these people will make the enforcement of the laws" since their voice is not socially isolated or politically mute, as is that of farmworkers. Providing food and clothing, visiting farmworker camps, and learning about working conditions, sheds light on these workers' hidden, ironic, suffering. However, shared experiences with farmworkers foster friendships and personal stories that can communicate to the separate world of citizens within North Carolina that these people are relatable, real, and suffering but can be easily helped and supported. Through the ministry's outreach efforts, Father Rafa is proud to admit that CMFF has "received many visitors. [They] came one week, and I try to give them a special feeling when they come here because I told them 'this is the CMFF but if you want this one will be your ministry' because you can help" and continue to spread the "special feeling" of belonging. In doing so, the ministry hopes to become the common ground, a home, to both farmworkers and outlier communities.

CMFF: Annual Farmworker Fair

> FATHER RAFA: "And we must understand that we have this treasure of people that provide us that we need to live for that reason we need to treat them with all consideration that they are supposed to receive from us. They are not slaves, they are not no different, they are the same. They feel, they live, they are afraid, they enjoy, they become sick, they will die."

Meeting basic needs and feeling cared for create a more comfortable atmosphere; however, they are not the sole foundations of community or home. Father Rafa instilled that his home "is full of love; full of happiness" and *that* is what he works to share with farmworkers and domestic residents through the ministry's annual Farmworker Fair. I was able to attend the Fair in the summer of 2008, and the level that Father Rafa had *not* been exaggerating in terms of the magnitude of the celebration amazed me.

My membership in a university student group that focuses on farmworker empowerment and support, as I previously mentioned, is what originally connected me to Father Rafa and the CMFF. I had visited the ministry facility, and listened to his description of the Farmworker Fair, as well as his hope that it would include at least eight thousand people. I considered this a gross overstatement, and maintained the image of a small-scale gathering of a couple hundred people with some music, simple children's games (probably including wading pools and face painting), and food. Basically, I drove to the Farmworker Fair expecting something along the lines of a church gala. As our four cars of volunteers crept along the grass fields that had been converted, through picketed flags and orderly lines of busses and cars, into an expansive parking lot, I was confronted with the absurdity of my mistake. What I had remembered as a quaint building surrounded by yellowed grass fields had been converted into a bustling core of festivities.

Soccer fields served as the median between the fair activities and the parking lot. An entire tournament made of teams from farmworker camps, church groups, and other communities, competed for prizes of calling cards, the family once again being a primary focus of CMFF activities. Father Rafa believes that sports, like celebrations, promote community: "When I c[a]me here, I used the sports to reach the farmworkers and I went to the camps, I played soccer with them, I played volleyball with them, I played basketball with them, and we, I get in a special mood. Like a family." During the fair, Father Rafa was the honorary referee for the semifinals and final game. The whistle he carried around his neck was tooted throughout the afternoon to attract attention to the flow of activities such as puppet shows for children and traditional dancing to live music. Different aid organizations were represented in stands that offered information about health care, childcare, legal aid, and other opportunities. Individual booths sold snow cones with chili powder, grilled corn with queso, and other regional food specialties. The ministry provided an endless supply of hotdogs and hamburgers, which volunteers such as our student group cooked and served to a continuous line of attendees.

Everything that was provided by CMFF (hamburgers, lemonade, hotdogs, music, puppet show, tournament participation, a moonbounce) was offered as a free demonstration of appreciation; the reciprocated gift that CMFF and Father Rafa received were the smiles and laughter of families, friends, employees, and employers celebrating together. Subliminally, connections are formed and strengthened by celebrating together "because we need to use some special ways that we have to feel funny and happiness and relaxed and this is probably the best way we can" (Father Rafa interview). Birthdays, good news, holidays, are most often spent with those who matter most to us. Creating a feeling of belonging, unity, within the community of thousands that are joined together, at least for that one afternoon, the Farmworker Fair reflects the respect for "interdependency, rather than solely...individualistic quests for opportunity and self-advancement" that link agricultural laborers and domestic communities (Susan Bibler Coutin). Communities inside, outside, and straddling the border of the agricultural lifestyle intermingle for a sole purpose. Once again, CMFF is in the midst of this unity; they continue to push the limits of their outreach to create friendships and community across assumed boundaries. Father Rafa explains that, "yes, CMFF is a home for the farmworkers," but that through outreach to communities that do not originally participate in agricultural activity, they can share and expand the family of this home. Battling isolation with festivity and education, Father Rafa explains that each added member to the CMFF family, regardless of background, is a step closer towards achieving home, "and for th[at] reason I can say you, Koehler, I can say you this is your ministry, your ministry. Keep us in your mind."

Concluding Words

Father Rafa's narrative depicts all three concepts of home within the farmworker community. His emphasis on living conditions and isolation are based on his desire to create a "home away from home" for farmworkers with living in North Carolina. This entails supporting, comforting, providing, caring, and treating farmworkers like humans, individuals, and ensuring that their humanity and emotions are considered before the service and labor that they provide. Programs such as the Farmworker Festival create the "home away from home" by encouraging community between farmworkers and domestic North Carolinians since "it is during fiesta…that issues of belonging, home, nationality, and affiliation are expressed most intensely" (Steve Striffler 2007). Father Rafa and CMFF struggle to break through the isolation and misconceptions that engulf farmworkers in North Carolina by creating opportunities for farmworker and outlier communities to mingle. However, Father Rafa maintains that family, either its creation or support, is the number one goal of migration, which therefore reflects their commitment to family values and emphasizes the humanity of their actions. CMFF extends avenues of communication between H-2A workers and their family abroad to sustain the memory and image of a cherished home that strengthens resolve and spirit. CMFF programs such as childcare support the third concept of home for the future within North Carolina.

Case Study #2: Fito and Arturo

Introduction

At the end of my interview with Father Rafa, he offered his assistance in locating farmworkers that I could interview. My investigation was limited to a time period that does not coincide with the North Carolina harvest season, and therefore there were very few farmworkers to contact. Any participating workers in the H-2A visa program would have been in their country of origin between mid-October and March if they upheld their contract, and therefore unavailable for interviews. The only possible pool of farmworkers that I could interview were consequently undocumented since they have no obligations to return to their country. To make matters more complicated, the trends of undocumented workers lead in two general directions that posed greater difficulty in contacting them for my interviews. Both trends concern the nature of their employment, with the assumption that this is the initial attractive attribute of North Carolina; undocumented workers may choose to "settle out" and find a non-seasonal job outside of the agricultural sector, or they may follow the harvest in a cyclical fashion throughout the Southeast.

As previously explained by Father Rafa, agricultural labor is not always appealing to those who come to the U.S. as farmworkers, but rather may be the only avenue that presents immediate job stability. Whether the individual came to North Carolina through H-2A or without a contract, the bustling cities' construction and poultry plants provided enough stable, non-seasonal, employment opportunities to attract farmworkers to exchange occupations and the migratory lifestyle for permanency. I chose not to pursue interviews with settled-out immigrants who were no longer affiliated with agriculture in order to concentrate the focus group of my thesis. Already, "male farmworkers" encompass a population that spans across a range of cultures and original countries, to include other modes of immigration would be too magnified of a project given the amount of time I had for my thesis.

If agriculture appeals to the individual so that he does not seek work in other economic sectors, then the migrant worker must circulate the region to follow the harvest and employment opportunities. Residing in a single location throughout the entire year is unfeasible for the majority of workers who hope to maintain employment. Agricultural job availability directly coincides with the harvest; additionally, if they are members of a crew of workers, then the decision to travel not only ensures employment, but camaraderie as well. The two farmworkers that I was able to interview, Arturo and Fito, had once cycled through the Southeast (covering areas between Florida and Virginia) until "the little ones began to come; the children."[6] They were able to find job opportunities that allowed them to remain in the same area permanently, and begin to establish a home. As a result, the narratives of Fito and Arturo are unique in the sense that they are undocumented farmworkers who have established a permanent residence in order to ensure stability for their family. Their actions reflect that, 1) the creation of a family was the reason for their initiation of a sedentary lifestyle and, 2) the decisions for their present are based on providing the best future home for their children and family but, 3) they still regard agriculture work as the employment of their choice.

Why Farmworkers are Here

My interview with Fito and Arturo provided a first-hand account that complemented the background research I had been doing on NAFTA and U.S.-Latin America relationships. Whereas Father Rafa alluded to the importance of employment opportunities within a farmworkers' decision to come to the United States, his main concern centered upon how to accommodate them once they had already made that decision. Hence, much of his narrative was directed at workers' rights and living conditions. Fito and Arturo, on the other hand, put the upmost focus on the availability of jobs. Only when they were prodded by direct questions concerning conditions by Elias[7] did they elaborate on possible infractions of worker justice or poor conditions; however, this was never in reference to their own situation. In fact, Arturo was very adamant in ensuring that his *patrón* (boss) was supportive and sympathetic. Answering my question of whether the farmworkers felt appreciated by their boss, the grower, Arturo explained, "more than anything he has supported us, too. With

---

[6] All quotes from interviews with Arturo, and Fito have been translated from Spanish to English. I have done this on my own, with help from Spanish Professors in order to best convey terms or phrases that I may not have fully understood on my own.

[7] Elias was the third person I interviewed, but the first person that Father Rafa referred me to. He initiated contact with Fito and Arturo, who trusted in him because of their hometown connections and the relationship that they had built through family and work.

work. And he opens avenues; with friendship, and care, compassion. He supports us when we need him, he is with us."

Arturo conveys a deep-rooted appreciation for the opportunity to work, "make a living," that is made possible by the grower. Both farmworkers came to the United States "for nothing more than to work," provoked by the economic barrenness of their own country (Mexico, in the cases of Fito and Arturo). Experiencing the unavailability of stable employment resulted in their vision of home that is contingent upon job opportunities. The farmworkers' position that "the only thing that you can ask for is that there is work" affirms the statistics concerning the impact of NAFTA upon accessible opportunities to support a family within Mexico. In February 2009, the U.S. (citizen) population without a highschool degree had an unemployment rate of 12.6%, whereas 4.1% of the population with a Bachelor's degree or higher were unemployed (US Bureau of Labor Statistics). During the same month in Mexico, 10.2% of the unemployed population age 14 and older had not completed primary education, whereas 30.84% had achieved a college degree (INEGI). Concurrently, investment of time, effort, and money to receive an education does not provide subsequent "avenues" of employment, as is the (general) case for U.S. college graduates; employment in the U.S. can therefore be utilized as a method of survival for the present and an opportunity for the future.

The determination expressed by Fito and Arturo towards pursuing stability and hope for the development of a future home affects the manner in which they consider their situation in North Carolina. Balancing the alternative of steady work presented in the US to the lack of work in Mexico is in the forefront of thought, rather than justice and belonging versus injustice and hostility, which serve as secondary concerns. Fito and Arturo attest their response to the question, "can a burden be lightened by a heightened meaning it acquires," by shouldering negative consequences of working in the U.S. with the hope of providing a better home and future for their families (James Peacock 2007:7). However, their particular circumstance supplies them with an additional component that may "lighten the burden" of working in the U.S. under hostile conditions: they reside permanently with their nuclear family. This option is relatively unavailable to the majority of farmworkers; hence the ability to feel at home, already tested by oppression, is increasingly challenged by loneliness and separation. Met with hostility and anger for "stealing jobs," and other such socially woven infractions, Fito and Arturo are able to maintain their pledge to pursue their home by "continuing to struggle, work. With a little or a lot, to *salir adelante* [come out on top, persevere]…hope that there is work to survive, to live."

The Undocumented Option

The H-2A guestworker visa program was implemented to encourage agricultural employers to legally hire international workers. Although this program has been successful in some sense, growers who use it are guaranteed laborers for their harvest season, this option is not perfectly implemented in Latin American countries. When I asked Fito why he had chosen not to participate in H-2A, he responded, "Back then, over there, you hardly heard anything about this, that people came with contracts. When we heard, we already were here [in the U.S.]. But, when we came that wasn't [available] in Mexico." Already, there are more Latinos that apply to the H-2A program than can be hired by growers in the U.S., yet, according to the U.S. Department of Labor, 53% of U.S. farmworkers are undocumented. People such as Fito and Arturo heard of employment opportunities through different avenues: streams of Latino migration have "destinations already determined through home-village networks" and although Latino presence is decidedly less conspicuous and established in North Carolina than it is on the West Coast, communities have developed over time that further encourage or facilitate continued migration (James Cobb and William Stueck 2005:82). Lack of documentation always the threat of being uprooted and sent back to their country of origin. However, the fact that H-2A visas are not presented or known in all states of Mexico, let alone Latin America, is coupled with additional incentives that undocumented immigration offers.

Firstly, it should be addressed that information and advertisement of employment surges south at the same rate that immigrants pursuing job opportunities flow into the U.S. Individuals who migrate to the United States are not specifically doing so in order to evade social obligations, but rather upholding them in a certain sense. Duty to provide for a family, offer a better future, become a benefit to society, pushes unemployed Latinos to the U.S.

H-2A workers must return to their country of origin after each harvest season. Therefore, the monetary investment generally cycles back to the hometown community; the pictures that farmworkers showed Father Rafa of houses and schools attest to this slow,

46

steady development. Despite public demonstrations of border control and immigrant regulation, "selective enforcement of the law –coordinated with seasonal labor demand by U.S. employers (as well as the occasional exigencies of electoral politics) –has long maintained a revolving door policy, whereby mass deportations are concurrent with an overall, large-scale, more or less permanent *im*portation of Mexican migrant labor" (Nicholas De Genova 2002:433). Undocumented migrants are not required to return home after the season; contrastingly, the journey back home is equally dangerous, expensive, and difficult to repeat multiple times if at all. However, the established nature of undocumented migration is that, through previously established channels, congregations of workers from the same hometown form labor crews that maintain the community unity, and migrate together throughout the Southeast as a complete entity so that "community endures even as the physical place itself withers" (Steve Striffler 2007:683).

Formation of these labor teams merely translate community ties across borders is not possible in H-2A labor camps. Although similar methods of advertising the guestworker program may exist, where news of employment circulates through families and hometowns, once H-2A workers come to the U.S., self-ownership is stripped and they become the equivalent of property. The grower selects the amount of workers that he needs and designates them to their camps. Some growers tend to rehire workers that exhibit "good work ethic," and may even take suggestions regarding family members; the final decision is always in their hands. Aid agency representatives have found it difficult to contact H-2A workers on some premises because of growers complaining of trespassing on their private property therefore placing farmworker personal right behind property rights. Isolation of workers is heightened in some situations by fences with "no trespassing" signs to intimidate and discourage visitors. To combat issues such as these, aid agencies argue for the farmworkers' rights as tenants to receive visitors. Appealing to the humanistic side of growers, that farmworkers are people who need socialization and have the right to mingle with other layers of society, had previously proved unsuccessful.

Contrastingly, undocumented labor teams maintain agency, on a group level if not as an individual, because they function under the authority of a "contractor," who many times began as a farmworker from the same hometown. The contractor, also called a crew leader, sets up contracts between the farmworkers and growers in search of agricultural labor.

Further the crew leader serves as an authority figure but speaks the same language and work in fields alongside farmworkers. Therefore, his role as an intermediary in language, rules, cultures, presents a more eased, gradually expected transition that fosters feelings of comfort and belonging. Undocumented farmworkers are under the care of the crew leader not only to find employment, but also housing, and basic needs. Overall, there is a more natural interdependence and community between work teams. Not only there more *choice* present in terms of who they live and work with, but a family-like atmosphere is created due to the shared past and connection to a home town.

Additionally, isolation of undocumented farmworkers is less stringent because of the crew leader position, which requires previous knowledge and interaction with established Latino and domestic resident communities in order to find work for his team. These interactions expand the web of interactions outside of the isolated camps, and can allow for the eventual opportunity of non-migratory jobs and conducive to creating a family. Undocumented migration is usually a decision necessarily accompanied by a focus on the future rather than the past. Policies emphasizing border control eliminate the possibility of ebb and flow between Mexico and the U.S., therefore constricting access to family, friends, and the life that remained in their country of origin. For that reason, farmworkers' investment is less likely to be channeled back to their country of origin because of the dubious possibility of returning to that life of their past; effort is instead exerted in created foundations for a home in the future.

Challenges to Home

The setting in which I interviewed Fito and Arturo supported the root of Father Rafa's concern for the overarching geographic and social isolation that all farmworkers are subject to. Before my interview with Arturo and Fito, I met Elias in a Fayetteville McDonalds so that I could follow him to the camp. The camp was located at least 45 minutes outside of town, down a small highway with sideline houses sporadically imposed upon yellowed fields of grass with grazing horses or cows scattered throughout. The largest establishments we passed were three gas stations, all of them assumedly locally owned, the closest to the camp being the *Doña Maria*. We pulled off of the highway onto a gravel road that we jostled along for about a mile past the house and treeline that greeted highway travelers until we reached a clearing. In this clearing were several trailers, a greenhouse for blueberries, and sprawling tilled fields. The situation of this camp is not unlike many others; geographic isolation from the outside community of domestic residents, along with the added bonus of living amidst the fields, allows farmworkers to perform their "sole function" of agricultural labor without any distractions.

Social separation of farmworkers consequentially promotes an atmosphere of uneasiness and discomfort stemming from the lack of interaction that allows for the proliferation of stereotypical slander. Arturo asserts, "The *hispanos* did not come to rob. They come to work," in response to a question of hostile assumptions that the farmworkers must struggle against while in North Carolina. Arturo and Fito accept the geographical isolation that is required for their job because stability of employment is their initial concern, yet this sacrifice is lost to the majority of domestic residents due to misunderstanding encouraged by stifled interactions.

Upon considering immigrants from Latin America, social and political tendencies are to clump together all populations and label them in a way that both demonizes their intentions and neutralizes any humanistic appeal or cultural identity that they carry. The term "Mexican" is used loosely to compress all immigrants from Latin America: with or without documentation, education, history, or actual affiliation with Mexico. Further, the synonymous "Mexican" and Latino immigrant population has been objectified and twisted into an issue that threatens social order and economic stability. The inaccessible communication between Fito, Arturo, and the members of the county in which they live allow for this demonization and objectifying actions to occur without remorse, and therefore concerning threats to the livelihood of farmworkers are hidden beneath the hubbub of amplified fears of change. Sofia Villenas notes that more than just the struggle to make a living, a "required resilience in the face of public discussion about Latino as 'other,' 'problem,' and 'noncitizen'" is immediately imposed upon migrant agricultural laborers (Edmund Hamann 2001:17).

North Carolina politics have engulfed the hostility between immigrant farmworker and domestic resident populations and solidified them in a series of actions that directly challenge the formation of home. Policies concerning "immigration control" and access to education reveal a primary focus on the possession of documentation as proof of legitimacy.

49

Legitimacy in terms of being a "legal" person, being a person at all rather than a "problem," and in terms of deserving acknowledgement for contributions. Richard Handler notes that "nations and ethnic groups provide their existence and their worth to the entire world by cherishing their property," with references to culture being arguably considered as property; with documentation being the contingent factor on which these policies revolve, the idea of a farmworker, an immigrant, as an object is sustained, stripping them of cultural identity and ownership (Brett Williams 1991: 65). The qualms of substandard living conditions, social justice, and health infractions are hence quietly erased from the public conscience since legal documentation trumps the importance of contribution, dedication, investment, or sacrifices made to establish a life.

In addition to encouraging public hostility and thwarting communal compassion, public policies such as 287(g)[8], which allows police officers to act "in conjunction" with Immigration and Customs Enforcement (ICE) officials directly challenge the ability for Latino immigrants to feel at home (www.ice.gov). Local law enforcement has the authority to detain immigrants who are not about to produce documentation even if no additional crime has been committed. Fito describes the fear of a father in reaction to ICE raids in admitting, "we hope that something changes... with the raids, all of that, because as you see on TV, they are deporting many, many people and the children must remain here, alone." A study on Mexican origin fathers uncovered that "immigration status was reported as a great source of stress and uncertainty for illegal immigrant fathers, which is turn influenced their level of involvement as fathers," and hampers the development of a home and family (Andrew O Behnke et al 2008:197). Children have been left on the side of the road after an officer, complying with 287(g), took their mother to jail for not having a driver's license. In February of 2009, the American Civil Liberties Union (ACLU) worked with the Immigration and Human Rights Policy Clinic at the University of North Carolina, Chapel Hill, to explore the effectiveness of 287(g) as comprehensive form of immigration reform and identified several problems (as well as offering solutions) to the policy. They cited "serious erosion of community trust" among Latino populations who felt reluctance to report witnessing or being victims of crimes out of fear of deportability; further, racial profiling was reported and an

---

[8] Section 287(g) of the 1996 Illegal Immigration Reform and Immigrant Responsibility Act (IIRAIRA)

overall ambience of "community insecurity" and uneasiness was evoked (UNC School of Law).

Attacking the future family of settled out farmworkers and other undocumented immigrants has extended to eliminate options for socio-economic advancement. One bill titled, "Community Colleges Can't Admit Illegal Aliens" was recently introduced to the North Carolina Senate with the hopes of legally barring community colleges to accept otherwise eligible students (acceptable grades, completed highschool, paying out-of-state tuition, unable to use federal scholarships) without documentation. The rhetoric of such bills, labeling the immigrant individual as an "illegal" being automatically alerts the public apprehension that this community's entire existence is inherently wrong, "against the law," slackens public compassion, and alerts wariness. Further, domestic residents jump to arms in defense of their own children, legal citizens, whom they perceive to be threatened by allowing "cheaters" take their spots within university systems (Di-Phi debate). Common tendencies of defensive domestic residents to depict "international migration of noncitizens as an illegitimate practice diminishes the human suffering experiences by the poor and unemployed...worker and refuses her or him the right to alleviate this condition through migration" (Harald Bauder 2006:32). Understanding the motives, history, and reason for immigration are secondary concerns to the immediate underlying fear of an unknown, "illegal," population.

Paradoxically, the same complaints of Latinos being drug or alcohol addicts, abandoning their families, and stealing jobs and social benefits from citizens are being more easily realized with such anti-access to education bills. Young children immigrating with their parents, after having received a highschool diploma, promptly have their future curtailed and restricted to jobs that do not demand college-level education are restricted to decidedly less opportunity to excel, better one's own situation, and reach full potential of social contribution. Not only are highschool dropout rates encouraged (why graduate if there is not another level to attain/pursue and these last years can be spent working), but a permanent secondary social class is accordingly created. Children who are brought to the U.S. with their (undocumented) farmworker parents present a high likelihood of continuing agricultural jobs if college is to be prohibited, therefore continuing to perform the necessary function within our society that systematically warrants no acknowledgment. Farmworkers who dedicate their present labor and sacrifices towards the pursuit of a future home for their family within North Carolina are being directly targeted by such policies.

The Undocumented Farmworker and his Family

Arturo and Fito's description of home supported the emphasis on family within a farmworker's life that Father Rafa had insisted upon. Arturo immediately answered, "Family is home," which the actions of Fito, too, demonstrate. Nine years ago, Fito came to the United States without a family and without a visa to pursue agricultural work. He followed the harvest and worked on farms in Florida, Virginia, and North Carolina. Presently, Fito lives with his wife and three kids in a trailer located in close proximity to the blueberry greenhouses that he cares for during the off-season. The added front porch, chickens, cats, dog, and pig that were scattered around the trailer's lawn testified to the permanency of their residence. When I asked him about his family, he told me, "We are six years old." Fito personifies, perhaps, the innermost fear of domestic residents concerning immigration because his kids, born in the US, are now citizens, and roots of permanency have been sprouted. Although Fito referred to his family remaining in Mexico, and wanting to visit them "some day," questions concerning "family" or "home" produced unhesitating answers focused on his nuclear family, only.

This alludes to an interesting phenomenon, of newly formed Latino families being forced to become increasingly nuclear, and mirroring contemporary "American" families of the United States. Farmworkers such as Fito do not have the option of returning to their family in Mexico, and therefore focus all their energy, hopes, and aspirations onto their children: working towards an idealized future home; the American Dream revamped. Within the United States, independence is considered a virtue that, on one level, is reflected in the fragmented family-life with high concentration on the nuclear members. This can be attributed to encouragement of offspring to follow their careers and dreams across the country; therefore, creating a life that is separate and distanced, geographically and eventually emotionally, from their roost. Immigrants such as Fito, who make a very similar choice to that of the independent "American" individual, are not similarly celebrated for their efforts to create a new, better, future.

The nuclear family emphasis has taken hold in the Latino community of the Southeast also due to the difficulty of migrating with one's entire family. Dwelling on families who still reside in their country of origin may be a tactic for H-2A workers to endure conditions of their employment, however immigrants who come without documentation have no avenue of returning without extreme difficulties, and therefore a focus on the future family and creating a new home is preferred and possibly healthier. Fito and Arturo, though they deny specific prevalence of this problem within Latino populations, agree, "one might [drink] when they feel alone," and when "they remember all the family." Fito and Arturo combated this loneliness through their emphasis on creating a future home with nuclear family. However, this decision resulted in a secondary isolation imposed by their retracted participation in cyclical migration practices: isolation from the farmworker/work crew community that continued to travel throughout the year.

The Undocumented Farmworker Camp as a Community

Camaraderie between farmworkers tentatively exists and offers a community or "home away from home" that "is grounded in a common experience of displacement and fractured reality," considering the blend of exclusion from outlier communities and the close quarters in which farmworkers must live (Steve Striffler 2007:685). Within camps, agricultural workers represent a medley of hometowns and countries of origin. Fito described:

We have shared, a little friendship with them working. Or, with them, we *work*, so we ask them how it is over there in their country, they tell us that it's a little bit more difficult...for them it's difficult as well so we come here...Struggling, searching for life.

The mutual tribulations faced in the fields as well as stories and reasons for immigration serve as a uniting factor within camps. However, Fito confesses, " some friendships continue but many go to other places, and then they end." The inscrutable future of a migrant worker whose location is, at least initially, determined by where the job leads them is a heavy challenge to the development of friendships that endure the continuous flow of seasonal work. Perhaps this, too, explains the collapsed distance of family concentration. With the primary focus being the nuclear family, the mobility of an agricultural workers' job causes less pain of constant separation from extended family.

However, the sentiments of Arturo and Fito may be distanced somewhat from the majority of undocumented farmworkers. My ability to have an interview with them was only possible because of their permanent residence in North Carolina; something that Father Rafa explicitly described as rare during the off-season. Pursuing the future ideal for their family, Fito and Arturo chose permanent residence in NC to allows for continued education for their children (U.S. Department of Labor reported in 2002 that the average migrant child who travels with their parents attends up to three school per years and consequently requires up to three years of education in order to advance to the next grade). Though they continue to live on a farmworker camp, they and their nuclear families are the sole residents for up to five months. Fito and Arturo place family in the forefront in their pursuit of a future home by choosing to settle in North Carolina. However, in Fito and Arturo's case, *community* as they knew it is no longer as feasible, since farmworkers come and leave each season, and domestic residents regard them with the indifference, at best, which is encouraged by their geographic seclusion and language barriers. Second generation children, therefore, can prompt a certain isolation from farmworker communities, but additionally "often [break] the crossing of boundaries for parents" imposed by "mainstream society" that initiates interaction with domestic communities (Caroline B. Brettell 2007:1). As a result, children, multiple generational investment, may prove to be the key towards actually accessing the ideal future home by gradually implementing the inclusion of the farmworker within U.S. society since "there are no second generation immigrants in the U.S. –they are all U.S. citizens" (Niklaus Steiner 2009:189).

Reasons and Benefits of choosing North Carolina

Referring to the future that he wants for his children, Fito describes, "that they study, that they do their best. But also that they learn about the fields." He strives to balance the agricultural heritage and roots of the creation of his family with the opportunity-filled future that education presents in order to prevent "heighten[ed] cultural boundaries between immigrant parents and their children" (Caroline B. Brettell 2007:1). The choice of ensuring a more stable environment for his family rather than adhering to the migrant lifestyle of his work crew community still carries heavy sacrifices; however, Fito's assurance that home is "with the family, the children, and work" reflects his confidence in his decision to settle out.

54

The consequences of permanent settlement ultimately benefit and strengthen the possibility of establishing a home for the farmworker family. Future generations of Fito's family will receive an education in the language of domestic residents. Not only that, but the children bear the first steps of integration of cultures; just by attending school, isolation between farmworker and outside communities is broken. Further, the education that Fito's children receive will eventually produce acknowledged contribution to society. The challenges to "home" of his past (Mexico's limited avenues towards survival/success without regard of investment towards education, etc) and present (U.S.' social isolation and lack of acknowledgment for his sacrifices and contribution) diminish with the generational advance and investment. Settlement and making his children's education and the comfort of his family top priorities are the best investments towards attaining a home.

Fito and Arturo experienced working and living conditions in states throughout the Southeast, and yet, six years ago, they chose North Carolina as, ultimately, the location of their prospective home. Fito explained that, "there is more support here; for the family" as opposed to other areas in the Southeast. When I asked them about the different agencies that had supported them in North Carolina, the only reference they made was of "the church:" CMFF. An additional implicit support network offered within North Carolina is his hometown community. The crew leader that first employed Fito also has his "home-base" in and permanent residence in North Carolina. Hence, the community surrounding the camp where Fito lives may have other settled-out farmworkers from the same hometown. Elias, for example, is the son of Fito's first crew leader and the godfather of Fito's eldest child. This reveals a glimpse of the intricate web of friendships and community that hometown affiliations maintain beyond merely working together as a crew. Choosing North Carolina as the state to establish his family in elaborates upon the significance that a farmworker's past and roots have on his decisions, even if the future is his primary focus.

The efforts of Father Rafa, too, provides comfort to Fito and his family at a level that was incomparable by any other Southeastern state. The first reference that Fito and Arturo made when asked about feeling welcomed in North Carolina was to CMFF, saying that there are "many people that...receive you well" and they "accept you a lot." Beyond family and work, Fito also described that one feels at home "when one lives well...without lacking [food] to eat." CMFF, through their visits to work camps, have been able to not only break through the rigid isolation imposed upon workers, but also to evaluate what is needed to make their employment more comfortable, and North Carolina more home-like. Fito remembers their deeds of "giving food... clothes, and, all of that, in the bags, the med-kits. All of that." The presence of support, welcome, community, that CMFF and home-town affiliations provides supported Fito and Arturo's decision to make North Carolina the location of their permanent residence and work towards "making ends meet, coming out on top; when someone comes from Mexico, they come with the dream to complete that." However, "as informants and as people on the margins, children provide just the kind of outlook and knowledge that encourages migration choices and facilitates migration once it takes places," such as settlement, creation, and investment in the nuclear family (Paula Fess 2006:235).

Concluding words

Fito and Arturo's experience within North Carolina demonstrate the actualization of the third concept of home: working towards an ideal home for the future. However, an important component in their understanding of home is also to be able to support oneself and one's family, the possibility of which is exacerbated by low job availability in Mexico to an extent that is not experienced nor comprehended by the majority of domestic residents of North Carolina. As a consequence there is a gap in understanding the motives of Fito and Arturo's migration from perspective of survival and striving to reach stability. To create stability, farmworkers such as Fito and Arturo accept the sacrifices of isolation from extended family and friends, social misunderstanding or contempt, with additional gratitude for the opportunity to work, provide for one's family, and set foundations for a brighter future for their children.

Fatherhood and the creation of a nuclear family provoked Fito and Arturo's decision to settle; however, the "home away from home" feeling of belonging that they found in North Carolina was provided through CMFF services and support of their family, as well as the hometown camaraderie they experienced with other farmworkers, crew leaders, and growers from their hometown in Mexico. Community within North Carolina was created between farmworkers by the histories of struggle that united them, the mutual appreciation and understanding of the present sacrifice with hopes for the future. It persists and creates a sense of belonging, home, almost in opposition to the misdirected labels of the North Carolina general public who do not incorporate gratitude, sacrifice, and family values into their image of undocumented immigrants.

Case Study #3: Elias

Introduction

Father Rafa recommended that I call Elias to get in contact with any remaining farmworkers during the off-season. I did call, and Elias, in turn, introduced me to Fito and Arturo, as well as sharing his personal narrative as a farmworker and aid provider. Elias and Father Rafa met in 1999 during one of Father Rafa's visits to a farmworker camp. Elias was working as a crew leader, and at the campsite with his crew when five vans drove down the gravel road towards the camp. He remembers the fear of the workers, who thought that it was an ICE raid, and so although he is a US citizen, he warily approached the vans. Father Rafa, however, popped out of one of the vans and comforted the workers, saying that he was only bringing food, clothing, and students from the University of North Carolina at Chapel Hill that wanted to visit the camp. Elias described how he had heard about Father Rafa, and the aid he provided farmworkers, but had never met him, so he went up to introduce himself. From that point, Elias volunteered to work alongside Father Rafa in supporting farmworkers around North Carolina and they built a "good relationship and as time went on and weeks went on and months went on and years went on [they] became carrots and peas" (Elias interiew). By 2007, Father Rafa approached Elias of behalf of CMFF and offered him a position as the youngest member of the National Board, and the first Hispanic member with agricultural origins; their hope that Elias' unique lifestyle of "living in two worlds, the American world and the farmworker world, [could bring] a better understanding and connection" between the two communities (Elias interview).

Elias's unique dual perspective as a farmworker in North Carolina and a citizen of the United States is a direct consequence of the 1986 "Amnesty Act," (IRCA) that offered "authorized legalization" for undocumented immigrants that had resided in the U.S. since 1982 (USCIS Immigration Legal History factsheet). The act also allowed seasonal agricultural workers who had performed at least three months of work during the previous year to apply for legal residency as well. Those who qualified for amnesty were additionally allowed to bring members of their families into the U.S. and pursue citizenship for them as well. Elias' dad had been in the United States since 1984 working as an agricultural employee of his brother, and eventually learning and growing to becoming a crew leader, and then a certified grower in his own right (as well as learning English and taking night school classes). His years of dedication to U.S. agriculture qualified him for amnesty; as a result, at the age of six, Elias and his three younger siblings were brought to the United States and granted permanent residency as U.S. citizens.

Elias' father accumulated farms in Florida and North Carolina with the understanding that "if you're really trying to pursue something, you have to struggle, and you have to really know how to spend your money wise[ly], and sometimes you have to sacrifice," which he had learned through his previous employment in a Mexican bank. Although Elias' dad graduated from the University of Monterrey and came from an educated, well-off, family, he did not want to follow the career path of his father, who was the mayor of their hometown. He felt an urge to have "everything he started from the ground up," even though his background did not require it. When he came to the United States, he knew the importance of beginning as a farmworker in the fields before becoming a crew leader or grower, so that he could "learn how it actually works" to grow North Carolina. Elias reinforces this mentality with his own children, too, having them work in the fields to keep connected and value the roots of their comfort, and telling them, "don't offend a farmworker, you don't humiliate a farmworker, you understand where you come from and thanks to that farmworker you're wearing the clothes that you're wearing, you're eating what made you grow up." I was attracted to the story and perspectives of Elias for the same reasons that he appeals to and useful to the CMFF board. Although he did not have a choice in relocating his home to the US initially, the bonds that he maintains with his farmworker origins and his drive to offer assistance, aid, and understanding to agricultural worker flocks offers rare insight on the blending and clashes of these two "worlds" and communities.

Why Farmworkers are Here

> ELIAS: "If they see their future, a brighter future, where they can accomplish that, in a different state, that's the person who migrates"

Despite Elias' family background of white-collar jobs and access to higher education in Mexico, his father still deemed employment in the United States as a worthier opportunity. His story distorts the assumed image that many U.S. residents have of immigrant backgrounds: that they were "worse off" in their country of origin and therefore bad conditions are more acceptable, less precarious to their health or offensive to their standards. Elias confirms that the goal of migration to the U.S. is "to go forward with their dreams" in a way that is not possible given the suffering economies of their country of origin. However, the attainability of home within North Carolina is continuously challenged; in fact, Elias confessed that although his house is in North Carolina, he does not "feel that connection [of home]; on the contrary, [he] feel[s] more challenging." He elaborates, that living in North Carolina, he has learned the "true meaning, the true definition, of 'stronger will survive' and what I mean by that is because if you're trying to move one step forward in what you're trying to achieve in your goals in your dreams, it's a challenge because there's always an obstacle." Even still, he "make[s] sure [he] really pursue[s] that happiness," and aids the pursuit of others, so that home will be attainable, and they can one day "taste" their accomplishment.

Elias cited a research study at North Carolina State University demonstrating that North Carolina farmers owning one acre of land can "get a gross income of $15,000. Not something to get rich, but it's something where you and your family can live." This mentality of "success" conveyed by Elias contrasts stereotypes by, 1) maintaining an agricultural mindset (therefore not stealing jobs) and, 2) focusing on "getting by," and supporting one's self and family in a more traditional sense and literally reaping one's life from the land. Elias claims, "we treasure America and carry America in our heart to the point that we sacrifice where we're coming from to reach America…So we feel more American even though we don't have a paper that says that." In elaboration, America presents the ideal home for immigrants because it ensures that their struggle will be for a *purpose*, with the promise that "the small little things can mean a lot if you really put in hard work and effort and believe in it" (Elias interview).

Migration to the U.S. occurs for the prospect that an American future offers: equal exchange of investment and return and a hope for future generations of their children. This goal is not selfish, is not based on stealing what does not rightfully belong to an immigrant, but rather repeats the actions of U.S. historical forefathers. The significance that "America" holds for Elias unites him with the original "American Dream" that has been taken for granted by a large part of domestic U.S. citizens whose memories no longer include eras such as the Great Depression, where struggle was required to "be somebody" and build up a life rather than have it provided. Niklaus Steiner remarks, "many scholars argue that the primary characteristic that forms a nation's identity is its attitude," however the "pull yourself up by the bootstraps" attitude of Latino immigrants that they believe encompasses the "American" identity has somewhat collected dust, and therefore poses more of a challenge to domestic residents than a uniting force (2009: 166).

Divided Latino Immigrant "Community"

Although Elias feels that Latino immigrants fit the mold of what is it to be American through their conscious struggles to "brighten their future," he notes that U.S. public reactions are anything but positive. Whether it is the clash of "old" verses "new" Latino immigrants, hostility from domestic communities, or the struggle within the "farmworker community," there is an overwhelming negative aura surrounding migrant farmworkers that reveals the effect of being labeled a "problem." Nicholas De Genova, commenting upon the division that results from public policies as well, notes, "one of the consequences… is that the sociopolitical category 'illegal alien' itself –inseparable from a distinct 'problem or 'crisis' …has come to be saturated with racialized difference and indeed has long served as a constitutive dimension of the racialized inscription of 'Mexicans' in the United States" that fractures any possible sense of unity (2002:433).

Discrepancy of "who belongs" is a divisive factor within the immigrant community. Leo Chavez notes that "one of the most difficult problems migration raises is how to think about culture and what happens as people move and mix;" U.S. reactions are to greet Latinos with an all-encompassing negative label of "Mexican" and "alien," thereby guaranteeing their "other"-ness (George Spindler and Janie E. Stockard 2007:293). Latino immigrants therefore feel pressured to define themselves beneath the sterile label and distribute legitimacy and character amongst themselves. Inability to distinguish imposed versus chosen and created identity results as they "encounter with established residents beliefs about their own identities, about the identities and beliefs of established residents, and about the political economy in which they are intertwined" (Edmund Hamann 2001:5). Being distinguished for superficial attributes such as language and skin tone rather than the seemingly subtle ethnicities, or even personalities, that create identity within all populations, renders impossible the fluidity and variety of culture and individualism of identity. Elias evaluates the Latino immigrant community as divided into three groups, Latino, Hispanic, and Chicano, whose inherently opposing identities threaten the possibility of solidarity and community due to their attempt to battle the imposed identity that U.S. citizens and policy assign.

Chicanos are U.S. citizens with Mexican parents who represent multiple of community investment and integration within the United States. Elias' children are Chicano, and he is Hispanic, a label that he defines as "people that come up from Mexico, in all different states of Mexico." Previous to the IRCA, the "registry date" of when an undocumented immigrant had begun his extended U.S. residence and could therefore apply for legal documentation was 1948; the act shifted the date to 1972, which allowed all immigrants who had entered the U.S. between 1948-1972 to apply for citizenship (US DOL factsheet). This included many of families on the West Coast; however, "when we decide who to include, we are also deciding who to exclude," and an exact divide based on newfound "legitimacy" between immigrants from the recent past and present as being was created (Niklaus Steiner 2009:173).

Elias' claim that "Chicanos, they just don't like Hispanics, and if you look on the immigration status, all the immigration patrol officers [on the Mexico-U.S. border], all of them are chicanos" materializes the animosity that he feels. Legitimacy that is arbitrarily imposed upon immigrant populations "as a distinctly spatialized and typically racialized social condition for undocumented migrants provides an apparatus for sustaining their vulnerability and tractability as workers" because it divides and amplifies hovering inconsideration of effort and dedication, thereby discouraging the fledgling immigrant farmworker population of North Carolina to establish an identity, community, and home (Nicholas De Genova 2002:439). The hostility that Elias believes to be channeled from the

Chicanos to new-wave immigrants is ironic and disheartening. The chicano movement incorporated liberation from oppressive U.S. social policies and attitudes that synchronized with their claim of belonging within U.S. society. Yet, new-wave immigrants who do not share this history of liberation and struggle for recognition within the U.S. are consequently excluded, and an additional obstacle is added to their quest to achieve belonging.

Chicanos, generally, credit high crime rates, drug use, alcoholism, and other negative attributes that have been assigned to "Mexicans" by domestic U.S. residents to the new wave of immigrants. Elias continues the trend by insisting that Hispanics "you are going to see working in the fields, working in [vegetable] packing houses, working in chicken houses," although they get blamed for "what [Latinos] do, especially with the stealing jobs…going to factories, construction…even working on fast food restaurants." He labeled Latinos as other Central Americans not originally from Mexico, however distinction is additionally rooted in how they pursue economic advancement within the U.S. Elias claims that while Hispanics pride themselves in *not* stealing jobs, but rather starting from the ground up, Latinos are equally ashamed of being groups with Hispanics, saying "I'm not the one being on the field, I'm not the mule, the working mule."

Whether or not these distinctions are universally acknowledged within the immigrant community from Latin America, it exemplifies the division that results from an assumed, negatively implied, identity. It should not be assumed that otherwise there would be perfect unity amongst all Latin Americans. On the contrary, Mexico, Guatemala, Honduras, Chile, are all different countries with separate cultural identities and values that distinguish them as equally as the many nations within the continent of Europe. However, hostility amongst farmworker populations diverts energy from being positively channeled towards making a home, creating a family, ensuring a better future.

Where do they Belong?

> ELIAS: "And to be honest with you. When I went back [to Mexico], those two times I went back, I never feel welcomed. And it's hard to say, I feel ashamed, but I just don't feel a home there anymore. I don't feel like, like you're welcomed

In 1997, Mexican Congress voted in favor of legislation granting the option to all persons born in Mexico after March of 1998 to apply for dual citizenship if the occasion should arise; additionally, all children of Mexican parents born outside of the country were granted dual citizenship as well. Previous to this action, any person migrating from Mexico and becoming a citizen of another country had their citizenship revoked. In the case of Elias and his family, the amnesty and citizenship offered by the 1986 IRCA, necessitated a renouncement of legal ties to Mexico. Although "in the United States, official models of naturalization presume that immigration consists of leaving one society and joining another," the question of whether the immigrant is actually welcomed and accepted into the U.S. remains (Susan Bibler Coutin, 2003).

Elias comments that whether or not you have documentation, "they call you an 'alien.' Which, you're not really an alien, you're just another person with different ethnic background." Assumedly, "alien" has been accepted within political discourse to describe a foreign immigrant residing in a country without legal documentation. Alejandra Castañeda describes how "through its language, [legislation] successfully contributed to an effect of estrangement, of othering, where migrants stopped being people and turned into real aliens, creatures far from human dignity," and therefore ""the solutions immigration laws propose reflect an approach to migrants as a negative aspect of U.S. life" (2006: 82,84). Fluidity between "alien" "Mexican" "illegal" and "immigrant" has concluded in the "one size fits all" label of anyone with brown skin and a certain sort of accent. H-2A workers, and families such as Elias', suffer from withheld "identity citizenship," which Steiner describes as "a sense of affinity and belonging" with the citizen population, although they may claim legal residence (2009:175). Elias explains that "even though they gave the H-2A workers temporary visas, they are the slaves of this generation," and their struggles have been discounted due to their association with illegal activities or persons, and therefore somehow deserved.

An example of the tenuous public understanding of farmworkers is exemplified through a non-profit group called "NC Listen" that claims to "be involved in immigrant reform and educating the public about immigration and its effects on America." Displayed on their online homepage, is a list of "immigration policy recommendations," the last of which is "No more 'Guest Worker' programs," referring to H-2A visas. However, within the descriptive paragraph to follow, this organization immediately identifies the problem as "jobs Americans use to do that are now being done by illegal immigrants." Intertwining H-2A workers and undocumented immigrants is a prominent mistake that not only taints the *legal* guest worker's dedication and contribution to U.S. agriculture, but also allows for a disregard that gravely endangers their lives. Father Rafa commented that farmworkers "come here to make a living, not to pay for [their] own funeral," yet this is not an unheard of phenomenon among farmworker families. Entire organizations have been created within North Carolina to prevent the simply avoided yet common death by dehydration because water is not always present or provided to workers in the fields. The threat of sickness and injury are intrinsic within agriculture, which the U.S. DOL identifies as one of the most dangerous jobs within the U.S; however, the threat is compounded by domestic public unawareness and concern for farmworker working and living conditions. Therefore, the social environment challenges the existence of farmworkers, let alone the creation of home, within North Carolina regardless of the service they provide, their humanity, or even the manner in which they migrated.

Apart from the social environment surrounding migrant farmworkers in the U.S., many also feel as though they no longer belong in their country of origin either. Father Rafa described the H-2A worker who returns home to a family that has grown and changed during his absence, and "vacuums" form in his heart. Elias, too, reveals the hurt of being misunderstood and a misfit in his original country, since he and other Latino immigrants are "the ones who are over here fighting, struggling, and they're treating you different and... you actually don't even belong over there anymore." In both countries, the struggle and sacrifice of a migrant farmworker has been ignored, with the primary focus being on the result; consequently, "what Hispanic immigrants learn within the United States is to view themselves in a new way, as belonging to Latin America entire –precisely at the moment they no longer do" (Daniel Arreola 2004:33). Elias testifies that a farmworker's primary identity becomes his occupation, and that his roots, rather than clinging to his country of origin, are burrowed in agriculture, since "This is how we started our life. This is how we clothed ourselves this is how we managed to educate ourselves this is a way of living." Therefore, despite tensions existing between countries or generations of immigration, belonging is found amidst the farmworker communities as they are "challenged to reinvent new narratives of group identities and solidarities (Edmund Hamann 2001:30). Similar to Arturo and Fito, Elias reflects that "the workers that I share in the labor camp I see them and they see me as one of their own, family."

> ELIAS: "To me, home, it's the place where I can go and rest, lay down, relax, forget about the
> world outside and be with the family"

Elias' actions as a farmworker, a father, and an aid agency provider exemplify the full scope of the answer to "what is home" to farmworkers in North Carolina. Home is volatile, meaning that it continually morphs, not only depending on the environment and culture that one is brought up in, but the environment that one creates. It is the ultimate ideal, created out of dreams and, for these farmworkers, in the face of disgust, shame, and triumph. Home, too, can provide the solution for closing the gap of understanding between farmworker communities and outside communities within North Carolina. Elias explains that unity is accessible between these two populations by "bring[ing] people to the labor camps…so that way they can build a good relationship with farmworkers so they can know that beyond the jar we've got *people* that are living in bad conditions." An inalienable right to "life, liberty, and pursuit of happiness:" to working without threats of cancer or death, to ownership of one's self and identity, pursuit of a better future: these have been denied to farmworkers, with or without documentation, and hence their right to a home has been threatened as well. Because of this challenge, the concept of home has morphed; why do they make their home in North Carolina? Elias' consideration of home in the camp and home as his family, as well as offering the possibility of creating a home to migrant farmworkers of North Carolina, demonstrates the way in which "home" inflates and constricts to best match an individual's blend of present, past, and future.

From the beginning of his immigration at age six until he was nineteen years old, Elias worked in agricultural migrant camps when he was not in school:

When I was younger we used to travel in different states and even though they were labor camps back then they were still considered to be my home. Even though I was in school and on the weekends I was in the fields, on the days off when there was no school I was in the fields. I was sleeping, too, at a labor camp in that little 16 by 16 space to be my room, my special place, my home, my shelter.

The farmworker camp was a place where Elias felt welcomed, belonging, because he was working with his family, and creating friendships with other migrants. Although the camp did not always include running water or private rooms for each worker, the main focus of Elias' time spent on the camps was in belonging, and therefore this was where he felt at home. This is not to say that conditions are not important, by any means. The experience of working and living in any place is certainly heightened by the environment, and Elias lived in conditions that *were not hazardous to his health or life* as many are that North Carolina farmworkers presently live in. Therefore, he was able to thrive and find happiness in the farmworker community, and thus felt at home:

The workers that I share in the labor camp I see them and they see me as one of their own, family. Take care of each other and look after each other. And I share emotional feelings, we learn how to become adults or we learn how to live in another world where we are misunderstood but we have to, people will just have to look at us to understand us and live what we live through and go what we go through so they can be able to understand us.

A key component of CMFF outreach that Elias emphasizes just as strongly as Father Rafa is the promotion of understanding. Adopt-a-camp is one service that offers farmworkers to experience appreciation, friendship, and care outside the boundaries of their camp. This service encourages congregations of churches, schools, universities, or clubs to create relationships with farmworkers. Although Elias felt "at home" in farmworker camps, his family was close by, and he worked with many people who came from the same hometown; not many farmworkers experience the same immediate connections, and, as previously discussed, are without immediate family. Adopt-a-camp provides an avenue to incorporate farmworkers into communities outside the camp, and offers, "just companionship so they won't feel isolated" (Elias interview). Elias explains that this is an opportunity allows for outside communities to gain not only knowledge of the origins of their food, the sacrifices behind them, but also to meet their neighbors, and "thank them for the hard labor, the sacrifice, their tears, their sweat, their humiliation. For providing that food on our table, it's just a way of saying thank you and 'we see you as one of us, as family."

Appreciation is a two-fold concept for Elias. Although acceptance and appreciation is key in feeling at home within North Carolina, Elias repeatedly conveys that, within the farmworker community and throughout the generations, it is important to appreciate one's roots, which he identifies as agricultural labor. Like his father, who knew the importance of learning to live off the land, a value that is no longer held as dear to white-collar domestic residents of the U.S., Elias believes that North Carolina "is how we started our life," making a contribution as accomplished individuals, and as farmworkers. Clothes, education, food, were made possible for his children through dedication to the land and working his way up with agriculture. Elias accepts that children are "pivotal to how a culture defines itself and its future," and therefore expects his kids to "pick up a bucket" and not only appreciate their origins, but incorporate them into their identity and home as well (Paula Fass 2006:7). Elias still struggles to bring "a change where we can actually be treated as human beings, not some type of animal;" however, through the values he has instilled in his third-generation farmworker children, the farmworker family, the community of CMFF, and outreach to communities outside the farmworker sphere, he has been able to carve out a home to belong in.

Concluding Words

The narrative of Elias and Elias' father, who initiated migration to the U.S., depict determination, drive to better oneself, and maintaining family values through their decision to make a home in North Carolina. These characteristics are usually applauded within U.S. society, but within the farmworker and Latino immigrant population, they have been twisted and formed into an illegitimate, challenging, threat to domestic residents (as reflected by media, public discourse, social ambiance, etc.). Elias works to provide belonging and the option of self-sustenance to other farmworkers as well through his collaboration with CMFF, further proving the selflessness that actions to create home must entail. Not all reactions to public hostility are positive, but rather divisions have fraught the Latino population within the U.S. as Elias illustrated. This, in turn, hinders opportunities of empowerment, voice, for farmworkers and the Latino population as a whole so that achieving a sense of home, community, and belonging is made more difficult. In addition to finding a place to belong, Elias enforces the belief that home incorporates a balance of history, roots, understanding of one's origins (which, in his case, is the agricultural lifestyle) and the opportunities that sacrifices have provided for the future generations.

Recommendations for future research

Although the case studies of Fito, Arturo, Elias, and Father Rafa permitted a glimpse at the network of processes that lead to home-establishment of farmworkers in North

Carolina, the inclusion of more farmworkers would have benefitted my research substantially. Two focus groups that I was unable to include were H-2A workers and undocumented workers that continue to migrate with the harvest throughout the U.S. Southeast.

Both Elias and Father Rafa identified H-2A workers as those in the most need in North Carolina, of support, friendship, compassion, and protection. Including this population within my research would have been vital in demonstrating the function of CMFF within their experience of North Carolina, and whether the "home" sentiment that they hope to provide is ever achieved. Further, it would have allowed a more in-depth understanding of my second concept of home (a focus on a idealized memory of their home in the past, in their country of origin, towards which their work in NC is invested) than what was provided to me by Father Rafa.

Interviews with undocumented farmworkers that continue to migrate throughout the Southeast would have complemented the "other side" of Fito and Arturo's experience. This focus group could provide deeper understanding of how the formation of the nuclear family affects migration trends, and how children contribute and change the farmworker experience. Is the decision to settle contingent upon where the farmworker is once children enter the education system, or is there a distinct magnetism of North Carolina? The appeal of North Carolina, specifically, could be further explored due to their experience in other states. Are aid agencies and support networks such as CMFF factored into the decision of where to settle out? My research is biased due to the connection that all of my interviewees had with CMFF and each other, so perspective from other NC farmworkers would be beneficial.

Conclusions

I have realized through interviews with farmworkers of the past and present and aid providers that home, like culture, is not a " 'thing'…something that mechanically gets reproduced from one generation to the next," but rather malleable to environments, emotions, experiences (George Spindler and Janie E. Stockard 2007:294). Because of this, North Carolina, in itself, is not necessarily the motivator behind Latino farmworkers' choice to stay. Instead, it is the marriage of what is considered and cherished as "home" and the avenues that are provided to them to maintain and reach that ideal. Through my case studies, I was brought to understand that programs such as CMFF offer a level of comfort and welcome that is unique in the Southeast. Father Rafa's emphasis on the interdependence of family and home acknowledges the human cravings within every individual to find a social space in which they can "live the love." Although working conditions, proper wages, and political presence is of importance as long-term goals, my interviewees expressed to me the patience that is necessary in the pursuit of home because of the multi-generational rate of accessibility.

Recognizing that creation of a family is a deeper motive and stronger attracter towards permanent settlement in North Carolina than do economic motives would allow domestic residents to connect with immigrant communities through shared values. Fito, Arturo, and Elias struggle to balance appreciation for their agricultural roots with the opportunity that the future provides for their children. However, this future of possibility, livelihood, achievement is what their struggles and sacrifices of the present are dedicated towards. Latino immigrants and farmworkers have not aimlessly drifted into the U.S., but rather have been forcibly pushed by economic and social factors in their country of origin. The effects of NAFTA and other foreign policies render impossible the attainability of a stable future for a large majority of Mexico and other Latino individuals and families. Therefore, Fito, Arturo, and Elias perceive home to be woven from the farmworker community, nuclear family, and the promise of a better future; investment for a purpose, contribution with acknowledgment.

My interviews prove that family, in fact, demands sacrifices from immigrants such as enduring subhuman working and social conditions to provide dreams for the future or choosing relative isolation from farmworker and domestic communities to ensure family unity and children's education. Political and domestic fears of self-serving immigrants who calculate the best way to impose upon the balance of USA culture are hence contradicted. However, policies such as 287(g) and efforts to bar undocumented children of immigrants to access of higher education suggest that politicians and domestic residents have already perceived the importance of family. Rather than considering the emotions and humanity that are involved with farmworkers' presence and settlement in North Carolina, these policies continue to attack the formation of family and their cultural reproduction and inclusion into

U.S. society. This is reinforced by political and media-driven efforts to incorporate illegitimacy into the immigrant image; thereby trumping any connection that mutually held values may create. My thesis, in exposing and exploring the reality of the agricultural migrant worker's experience, offers a new education, from the perspective of an agricultural worker seeking home, that promotes united understanding rather than divided judgment.

Bibliography

Bauder, Harald
    2006 Labor Movement : How Migration Regulates Labor Markets. New York: Oxford University Press.

Behnke, Andrew O., with Brent A. Taylor and Jose Ruben Parra-Cardona
    2008 "I hardly understand English but..." Mexico Origin Fathers describe their Commitment as Fathers despite the Challenge of Immigration. Journal of Comparative Family Studies: 187-205.

Carlson, Laura
    2007, NAFTA, Inequality, and Immigration. Electronic document, http://americas.irc-online.org/am/4705, November 6.

Castañeda, Alejandra
    2006 The Politics of Citizenship of Mexican Migrants. Grand Rapids: LFB Scholarly LLC.

Coutin, Susan Bibler
    2003 Cultural Logics of Belonging and Movement: Transnationalism, Naturalization, and U.S. Immigration Policies. American Ethnologist 30: 508-26.

Coalition of Immokalee Workers
    2007, CIW Anti-Slavery Campaign. Electronic document, http://www.ciw-online.org/slavery.html, December.

Clark, Jonathan
    2005 Unemployment statistics don't tell the real story in Mexico. The Miami Herald, June 11.

Cobb, James, and William Stueck, eds.
    2005 Globalization and the American South. New York: University of Georgia Press.

Cole, Stephanie, ed.
    2004 Beyond Black and White: Race, Ethnicity, and Gender in the U. S. South and Southwest. New York: Texas A&M University Press.

Collins, Kristin
    2008 Tolerance wears thin. The News&Observer, September 7.

Collins, Kristin
>2009 Colleges could profit from illegal immigrants. The News&Observer, March 25.

De Genova, Nicholas P.
>2002 Migrant "Illegality" and Deportability in Everyday Life. Annual Review of Anthropology 31: 419-447.

Dickerson, Marla
>2006, Placing Blame for Mexico's Ills. Los Angeles Times, July 1. Electronic document.http://articles.latimes.com/2006/jul/01/business/fi-mexecon1, July 1.

Fass, Paula
>2006 Children of a New World Society, Culture, and Globalization. New York: New York University Press.

Fleck, Susan and Constance Sorrentino
>1994, Employment and unemployment in Mexico's labor force
>U.S. Bureau of Labor, Monthly Labor Review, November.

Gill, Hannah
>2006 Going to Carolina del Norte. Chapel Hill: University of North Carolina Press.

Hamann, Edmund
>2001 Education in the New Latino Diaspora: Policy and the Politics of Identity. Grand Rapids: Ablex Corporation.

Instituto Nacional de Estadística y Geografía (INEGI)
>2009, Composición de la población desocupada de 14 años y más...(Nacional). Electronic document,http://dgcnesyp.inegi.org.mx/cgi-win/bdiecoy.exe/617?s=est&c=12913, March 24.

Kandel, William A. and Emilio A. Parado
>2006 Rural Hispanic Population Growth: Public Policy Impacts in Nonmetro Counties *In* Population Change and Rural Society. William A. Kandel and David L. Brown, eds. Springer.

Larson, Alice C.
>2000 Migrant and Seasonal Farmworker Enumeration Profiles Study: North Carolina. Migrant Health Program, Bureau of Primary Health Care Health Resources and Services Administration.

Lock, Margaret M.
    2002 Twice Dead: Organ Transplants and the Reinvention of Death. Berkeley: University of California Press.

Migration News
    1998, Mexico: Dual Citizenship, Economy. Electronic document, http://migration.ucdavis.edu/mn/more.php?id=1426_0_2_0, January Volume 4 Number 1.

Migration Policy Institute and Population Reference Bureau
    2008 Immigration: Data Matters. Washington, D.C.

National Agricultural Workers Survey
    2009, The National Agricultural Workers Survey. Electronic Document, http://www.doleta.gov/agworker/report9/chapter4.cfm#plans_to_remain, January 13.

NC Listen
    Real Immigration Reform is Needed Now! Electronic document, http://www.nclisten.com, accessed January 2009.

Peacock, James L.
    2001 The Anthropological Lens: Harsh Light, Soft Focus. Cambridge: Cambridge University Press.

Peacock, James L., with Harry L. Watson and Carrie R. Matthews
    2005 The American South in a Global World. New York: University of North Carolina Press.

Peacock, James L.
    2007 Grounded Globalism: How the U.S. South Embraces the World. Athens: University of Georgia Press.

Redden, Elizabeth
    2009, Data on the Undocumented. Electronic document, http://www.insidehighered.com/news/2009/03/17/undocumented#Comments, March 17.

Spindler, George and Janice E. Stockard, eds.
    2007 Globalization and Change in Fifteen Cultures: Born in one World, Living in Another. Belmont: Thomson Wadsworth.

Steiner, Niklaus
    2009 International Migration and Citizenship Today. New York: Routledge.

Striffler, Steve
    2007 Neither Here Nor There: Mexican Immigrant Workers and the Search for
    Home. American Ethnologist 34: 674-88.

Student Action with Farmworkers
    2007 Facts about North Carolina Farmworkers. Fact Sheet. North Carolina
    Farmworker Institute.

Terrazas, Aaron, with Jeanne Batalova and Velma Fan
    2009, US in Focus: Frequently Requested Statistics on Immigrants in the United
    States. Electric document,
        http://www.migrationinformation.org/usfocus/display.cfm?ID=649.

University of North Carolina at Chapel Hill
    2006 North Carolina's Hispanic immigrants contribute more than $9 billion to
    economy, Jan. 3. News Release, 30. Chapel Hill: North Carolina Bankers
    Association, University of North Carolina News Services.

U.S. Citizenship and Immigration Services
    Legislation from 1981-1996. Immigration Legal History. Electronic document,
    http://www.uscis.gov.

U.S. Census Bureau
    2005 Geographic Mobility between 2004 and 2005. Census Report. Population
    Report of the United States: Dynamic Version.

U.S. Department of Agriculture: Foreign Agricultural Service
    2008, FACT SHEET: North American Free Trade Agreement (NAFTA). Electronic
    document. http://www.fas.usda.gov/info/factsheets/NAFTA.asp, January 16.

U.S. Department of Labor
    2009, Employment status of the civilian population 25 years and over by educational
    attainment. Electronic document,
        http://www.bls.gov/news.release/empsit.t04.htm, March 6.

U.S. Department of Labor: Employment Standards Division
    2009, Wage and Hour Division (WHD): H2A Compliance Review. Electronic
    document, http://www.dol.gov/esa/whd/regs/compliance/fmla/H2A.htm, April
    2.

U.S. Immigration and Customs Enforcement
    2007 Section 287(g), Immigration and Nationality Act; Delegation of Immigration
    Authority. Electronic document, http://www.ice.gov/pi/news/factsheets/
    070622factsheet287gprogover.htm, June 22.

Vallarta Rodríguez, Dr. José Enrique
2008, Unemployment and Mexico's Need to Create More Jobs. Electronic document, http://mexidata.info/id1722.html, February 18.

Walker, Marlon A.
2008 NC sheriff's slurs snarl local's immigration work. USA Today, October 24.

Wharton University of Pennsylvania
2005 Mexico Faces Up to Unemployment Growth. Electronic document, http://www.wharton.universia.net/index.cfm?fa=viewfeature&id=1026&language=english, September 25.

Wise, Carol.
1998 The Post-NAFTA Political Economy: Mexico and the Western Hemisphere. New York: Penn State Press.

Appendix

Father Rafa Interview

(Q:Koehler Briceño, A: Father Rafa)

Q: How do you define home

A: Okay, my definition of home is a family

Q: A family

A: A family where the parents and children can live together. This is a home.

Q: When someone says home, the word, is there a specific image or emotion or smell or anything else that comes to mind

A: Mm, eh, yeah, eh when we talk about a home we have, initially we have a place but, ehh, we can not, ehh, understand, eh, a home without a family living inside of this place. Ehh,

Q: Do you have a specific image when you think about your home, like a specific place or does it have to do specific, just with the family

A: Eh, love, respect, justice, peace, help, support, ehh, all, all that, spiritual expressions with the, what the, who live.

Q: Mm hmm, so where is your home

A: Where?

Q: Yeah

A: My home?

Q: Yes

A: My home is _____

Q: Mmhm, so that is a specific place

A: Yeah it is a specific place but it is full of love. Full of happiness, I feel really happy when I get home. I have my wife, my children visit me once in a while, but every minute of our life is trying to live the love. Every minute of our life we try to do the best loving and respecting and helping and trying to do the best for the others.

Q: Do you think that a person can have more than one home?

A: Ehh, I, I, uh, I can say my home is my home. Es, to me my home is my home because, for example, I live in a place but in that place I, this is my home because all that I can have to live is with me under this, ehh, in that building. I can say I have children, and they have their own homes, but they are, these are their own homes, but not my home. My home is the place where I live and where I can have all that I need to live. Love.

Q: How did you find out about this organization CMFF

A: Eh, I can, I was working, I was a priest of the republic's dioceses. Once I knew that here in north Carolina the diosisis was looking for a priest to work I was in touch with the person that I knew in Puerto rico and I told her, if you want, I can go to north Carolina and work there, and I feel very priveledged because I could come to work here

Q: Why did you decide to become a part of CMFF?

A: Me?

Q: Yes

A: Eh, when I come here I didn't know the specific would be my work but I, I understood, ehmm, I understood that the work would be hard work. And I started to work. I remember that, especially when I came to work as a priest for the CMFF, I was working with the demoninational church and I am a priest, and I remember that when I came here I tried to introduce myself to the people here, especially to the migrants, and when I told them I am a priest, they didn't understand very well and some understood that we were not roman Catholics

Q: Yes

A: And, when they understood you are not roman catholic, they understood that this was not a true church because according to our culture we receive all spiritual and church information from the RCC and they say us the only one true church is the RCC and for that reason when I talk to the migrants here at the beginning and I told them I am a___ priest they were very afraid. And initially I felt that I was not welcome and, eh, and I tried. I remember that many times I told them I am _____, _____, and la iglesia _____ and they couldn't pronounce the word_____. "pis pis pis" right now they say there isn't a iglesia_____. And we worked very hard, very hard for years. And we had every Sunday twelve, eighteen people for months and years, more than two years. And, ehh, and ehh, I continue visiting places, camps, talking with people and I don't know how this place were full of people because, ehh, after three years I could see 7, 8 thousand people here and I asked myself "what happened?" I don't know what happened. I don't know what happened. But the reality that people love and enjoy very much to attend to the CMFF for its programs and for the services that we provide every Sunday for them and we continue growing up. I don't know why but we are all, I feel very happy when I can see that the farmworkers come here by, in their own busses, and I can see that in the busses there are 80, 90 people. And they come here, they enjoy it. And they say to me to come here every Sunday is to come to a party, we feel very happy.

Q: That's good. Um, how long have you worked for CMFF?

A: I have worked for 12 years

Q: What was your personal experience with farmworkers before you came here to CMFF

A: In south America I was ordained in 1962, I was a common priest 47 years ago. In Columbia I worked, I loved to work with people. I remember that when I was ordained I went to the bishop and the bishop told me "you will be, ehh, one of the más close..ehh..helpers" and I was working at the office. The bishop office, but I didn't feel well. And I told the bishop "I don't feel well working here" because I was sitting in an office and everybody bringing coffee, toast, and I didn't feel well. I, I , I told him that I needed to work with people and he told me "okay, you want" and I went as a chaplain of a college, a big big college. And at the same time I was chaplain of the army, and I had three churches in the mountains that I attend during the weekly and Sundays. I was very accustomed to work with the people who worked in the fields. To me it was not, when I come here, It was not a new experience. I was accustomed to work with people like this. Simple people. And, I was a sporty man. I played soccer very much and was an athlete. Track and field, I was in this, volleyball, basketball. All of the sports. And, when I come here, I used the sports to reach the farmworkers and I went to the camps, I played soccer with them, I played volleyball with them, I played basketball with them, and we, I get in a special mood. Like a family "oh, eh, father rafa, our friend" I remember that once, up there, a soccer game, some farmworkers came to me and they told me "this is the best, the happiest time that we have here during the whole time that we have been here" for that reason I try to give the love andi try to provide them some bread, some clothes, and especially, sports. I feel very happy when I can see, and I don't know how these people can do this, but when FW come from camps and 6,7pm, and before eating they go and they play soccer. I can't not understand (laughing) how these people working 12, 14 hours, can come here and play soccer. Because we need to use some special ways that we have to feel funny and happiness and relaxed and this is probably the best way that we can. And I don't know what, ehh, I want to say you this that when I came here, ehh, 12 years ago, and I visit the camps where the farmworkers live, I spent more than two years without resting well because, especially (voice breaks), during the night, I was trying to, to, to sleep, and I was thinking how these people can live in these camps. In these unhuman, unhuman conditions because they don't have any. They don't have shoes, they don't have underwear, they don't have a bed, they don't have chairs, they don't have a kitchen, they don't have privacy in a restroom, they don't have restroom, it is , they don't have any any any and they don't have family. And I, I , I couldn't imagine how these people could live and many times during the nights I wake up and I wake up and I am thinking how these people could feel and live in these camps because it continued being the same and they don't have any, any any. This places smell abd, bad, bad. Because there are some places that are supposed to be for forty people and they, the growers, accommodate there, 70 or 80 people and they have septic tanks, they cannot process all this, ehh, you can feel and you can smell the worse odors. Smell bad and with these odors, in this condition, people live. They eat. And they don't have the most elementary conditions to rest. They don't have a mattress, they don't have a pillow, they don't have anything. And you can see a picture, like this (motions to walls that are covered in large pictures of the inside of FW dwellings and FW resting, eating, etc inside). The reality of the camp.

Q: What is your personal goal, or the goal of the agency, regarding farmworkers:

A: We need, we need to reach people with power. People that can keep the loss. Ahh many time, I think, I am in a church, the ____ church, and I have seen many students, I have seen universities, I have seen schools, I have seen churches that come here. And we talk, we talk about the farmworkers, and how these people live. I remember that the…years ago I knew a professional photographer. He came because he was working for Newsweek. And, eh, he was in Durham and he called me and he told me "I know that you work with migrants, could I visit with your place where the migrants are" I told him "okay, I will be very glad to go with you" and he came and we visit some camps and I told him "these are some of the best camps" and he, he told me "it's impossible to believe that this is the best camps. If this is reality I need, please, to know the worst camps." I visit camps with him and he told me "I can not believe that people could live here in the united states in these conditions" and believe, they, I have seen some videos from Africa, and, that, I know that in Africa there are special places where the people suffer suffer suffer, very much but I saw some videos from Africa and I could conclude that people in Africa live in better conditions than the migrants. You can see. The migrants, the the number one for the migrant is his family. His family. I remember that once I visit the camps and I went, eh, morning hours, to a camp, I ask for a farmworker y the, the, camp makes, y they told me that a fire in his face because he was cooking in something and it burned his face. And I told where he is "I don' t know, I don't know" and I supposed that he was at the hospital. Then I came back to the camps at seven pm. This happened morning hours. And I asked for this farmworker and the camp makes told me "he is here" and he came and he was very very burned on his face and I told him "what happened" he explained to me. "Where you, eh, where you when I was here" and he told me "I was at the, Clinton, I was talking to my family on the phone" and I asked him "did you tell them, your family, what happened" he said "no, I told them I am fine." for them, to be in touch with their families is the most important. And, for the reason, this man was burned, this man was suffering, and he prefers to talk with his family than to go to the hospital. I took him to the hospital this night and he was for two days at the hospital. And, eh, this is too too too sad I can't imagine, I cannot imagine, how these people can live. And for the reason I can tell you the worst for any people, any man, and woman, is to be separated from their families, of course.

Q: Um, so, what are some needs or rights

A: Ah, you asked me about the goals, yeah, and I told you that we have people with power. We have lawyers, we have a very important people in our special churches. To reach them, they must know what is happening in our camps. They live in separate, isolated, they live like perfect slaves. They can not move, they can not be seen with visitation from friends or family. The grower don't let, don't let. And they have not kitchen they have not a room to sleep, they have not mattresses, they have not any any any any. And the most is that the growers are in imminent danger. The danger of dying. Because, eh, when the growers are working, they must work with the pesticides. And there are some pesticides and some chemics that are used for, for example, to get yellow color, for, eh, tobacco leaves. And for example poisons like this, pesticides like this are supposed to be sprayed into the fields and all farmworkers must be out of these fields for 48 hours. And there are at, in other states. Because I knew. Places where, after spraying this pesticide, they must put big sized announcements that reads "nobody can come here after 48 hours" and they put the day and the hour and what this pesticide was sprayed. And I knew here, when I came here, people that, after spraying this pesticide, they were pushed to go into the fields. When any farmworkers get this pesticide in his body, they would suppose that he would live five years. And I could see and I could here people that told me "we got this pesticide in our bodies" I knew a man that drive, drove, a tractor and told me "I was through the fields and I could feel these pesticides was in my body" when this pesticides took the body, this pesticides go inside and destroy all all all that is inside. And I remember that I, I could see some farmworkers and at that time I did not understand very well and some told me "father, I don't feel well. I don't feel well." I knew that these people got pesticides. I knew that they got. Especially because I knew them at Atlanta, not too far from here, they told me two or three years after. They told me "we don't feel well, maybe I won't come back this next year." And I am sure that they died. Because the poison was there. It destroyed them. What is my goal? My goal would be if I could see a law. Because we have the laws, we need the enforcement. We need this, I could see the enforcement of the laws that say in all camps of North Carolina where a pesticide was sprayed, we must put this announce, these signs that reads that nobody can come here. And we will save lives. I told the farmworkers. Because when they come from Mexico in bus at the grower's association. North Carolina Grower's Association building, they receive all information about the pesticides and how, what they are supposed to do. But they don't do any because they are afraid. If they don't go into the fields the grower will fire them. And I told them "if you see that a pesticide is sprayed and somebody told you go inside tell them no! I won't go. Because you come here to make some money, to live, no[t] to pay for your funeral." So. Don't go into the fields after spraying the pesticide. So many, I'm sure, go into the fields after they spray with pesticides. And they die. We make noise, we talk about the, the lethal weapons and something like this. And we have here, in our country, in our fields, lethal weapons. I, I do not want this. They are supposed to come to live, not to die. But they die. Many, many die. Because, the laws, for the growers and people with some material power, protects the people that have money, people that have camps. They don't take care of the farmworkers. They are slaves. And they will die.

Q: Um, what do you believe to be the main goal of immigrants who come to work on North Carolina farms?

A: The goal of the migrants is if they, they can have all facilities to be in touch with their families. I can see a, one camp, near Clinton. And that camp, I could see the migrant live like human beings. I could see they have pretty, beautiful building. They have a beautiful kitchen. They have refrigerator they have a great dinner place, with tables and all. They have eight public phones to make calls to Mexico, to their families. I have seen camps where they don't have any public phones and they are they must walk near one hour to get a public phone to talk with their families. And, my, the farmworkers I suppose that they will have an idea to reach a goal in the camps, a place where they can live like human beings. No, no like less than slaves.

Q: Um, why do you think that North Carolina, specifically, is a target for recent immigration? Like, people come to North Carolina to work?

A: they come here because there is the agriculture is the most important in this state. And they, this opportunities to come are offered to them in Mexico and they say "I can go there and I can work in the fields" and they are in our countries, in Mexico, in Honduras, in Nicaragua, there are many people that work at the fields in these countries. And there are many people that are not familiar with fields. Some of them are electricians, some of them are mechanics, some are work in computers, some are technicians. They cannot work in their countries because there is no job for them. And when they knew "we can go to north Carolina, to the united states and work in this special work, job," they say they will do it, "I will go," and many of them can not resist the work at the camp because it is too hard. They cannot. For the reason I have seen many farmworkers that are up there one week or two weeks working at the camps. They are sick, they do not feel well. And they say I cannot continue here because I will die here, I will go back to my country. And for the reason many come here because it is an opportunity. Some are familiar with this opportunity, some no. and for the reason some can handle this work and make some money that they will use and some, some say I can not stay here they go back.

Q: Do you believe that it is important for farmworkers to stay in contact with their family?

A: Oh, it is the most important. The most. And they, they, they try be, stay in contact, in touch, with their families. I am sure that each farmworker spend at least fifteen or twenty dollars in phone cards to make calls to their families.

Q: So, how do you encourage or administer help to FW who want to contact their families?

A: I am, I am thinking right now we have the, the, cellphone. I am trying to see if I can be in touch with a company for cellular phones. And. This ministry, because we are in touch with thousands, I think that this will, I have been in touch every year, o, between five, six thousand people. I visit camps where I can find two hundred farmworkers, 80, 50, 20. I am in touch with thousands and all are trying to be in touch with their families. And, maybe, you can tell me, we can make contacts with a company like AT&T, something like this, and have here, like, an opportunity to provide them this cellular that they can use during the time that they will be here. It will be great, great because they suffer very much because they don't have a cellular. Maybe could be hard for them to get this cellular, and at the camps they don't have public phones and they are uncommunicable. And I am thinking it would be great if we can have here, for example, two thousand cellulars, and "do you want, this is a contract, you can use this is this way and you can continue using." There are many ways, I don't know.

Q: Do you feel that their families have an effect on their experience in the United States? The families of the farmworkers, do they affect their experience in the United States?

A: Oh, yes. Effect in many many times positive, many times, negative. I have seen families that, with the job, the work, that the farmworker made here they can have more and better facilities in their countries. For example,I have seen, eh, some farmworkers that say to me they show me the pictures of their houses. Pretty houses. And they say "we could make this thanks to this work because we save money and we use this money to have better homes" and, eh, and they say "I have better homes but I have in my heart vacuums because I couldn't share with my children, my wife, and I lost the best time. The best times." And, and, I have seen some farmworkers that say, "I have spent nine years coming here. This next year I won't come because I, I cannot, I can not support one year more. One year more of come here and leave my family. No. I need to, to share with my children. I need to, to recover the lost time with my family and I can't." I have seen farmworker that say I came here and my family was destroyed because my wife is in love with another man. She was alone. And this can happen. Some can lose this to have a better condition. Some can say " I can to north Carolina trying to have better life and was not was it was. Destruction."

Q: How many farmworkers do you think have their family with them, here?

A: That have his family here?

Q: Uh huh, or family in the united states

A: No I can say you for north Carolina, eh, no not many. Not many families, no. not many families I can see no, not many.

Q: So the farmworkers that do have they meet them, they meet their wives, or they make their families back at their country of origin or here

A: Yeah, there are some, like I told you, some that the man come here and they go back to their. And there are thousand thousand of farmworkers that are here for eyars. Five, six, seven, ten years separate from their families.

Q: So do you think that most farmworkers in north Carolina, at least, are, they're not made in north Carolina, they're made back

A: Yeah and especially. We have here in north Carolina, for example, on right now there are no farmworkers here. Only a few but the most part of them were moved to other states. And they continue doing this for years and years and years. Four months ago I met a man in Goldsboro and he told me, and I knew him when I came here I knew him about ten years ago. And he told me "father I came here because I want to say you hello because I will come back to my country. I can not support one more day here." Antero, his name is Antero, I met him and he say I can, so, "I will go to Mexico to meet my family. And I don't know what I will find." It's terrible. Terrible.

Q: So, have you noticed any trends with workers who try to stay in the United States after the harvest season?

A: Eh, no.

Q: Like, why do some farmworkers stay after the harvest?

A: Yeah, there are here in this side of NC only a few, only a few, farmworkers who stay here. Why? Because there are, 99% of the camps are closed. And, eh, they will reopen on April, May, or June. And, eh, the farmworkers, they must to go to other states. And the H2A must to go back to their countries. And for the reason, they must. A farmworker's family divide. Like I told you I know three womens or four womens who are here with their children because they are studying. And the husband, they move to another state to work with the contractor and they are separate. We have only a few farmworkers that we work. For example, at the......blueberry...only a few that work at the blueberry and they are here with the families. At only a few, the rest are all at other places. And I will see women that, the husband move to another state, and the womens, the wifes, are here and they will work at the blueberry. But we have not families here. They are divided. Divided. And only a few, a few, like.....and the three or four workers that they have, they will continue here. Only a few few few.

Q: So, over the summer when there are a lot more farmworkers here, do they interact much with the workers that stay year round. Like those families that are here year round, over the summer when the other farmworkers come do they interact much, do they, are they with each other?

A: Oh yeah, absolutely because they meet one each other

Q: Do you think any of them ever encourage them to become part of their community? And stay in North Carolina after the harvest?

A: No because they, eh, many times I ask myself how these people want to a different work. No? I know some men and they are my friends and they work in construction. And some of them told me "do you have some people that need work and want to work with me in construction?" and, they tell me. And I remember that I talk with some and some of them told me "we love to work at the camps. The agriculture" they love, they love. And some told me "okay, I will" especially with people that I have some relationship and I know them very well and I can give them some opportunities to improve their living conditions and for the reason I talk with them and "if you want, you will have more money you will stay more relaxed, you will have safety, water, you will be more safe" and I have heard that some of these people they went to work in the construction and they are strong men and they came back to the camps. This is a vocation, I don't know, maybe you will be an intellectual, professional, and this is your vocation. And these people say "no, I love the camp. I love the agriculture" and my deep confusion is this. God gives to each one a gift. And thanks to the gift we can live because if we won't have farmworkes we will die because we won't have any to eat. And for the reason they are farmworkers. And they love it. And we must understand that we have this treasure of people that provide us that we need to live for that reason we need to treat them with all consideration that they are supposed to receive from us. They are not slaves, they are not no different, they are the same. They feel they live they are afraid they enjoy they become sick, they will die. I feel that I gave you the answer.

Q: Um, so, do you think that NC becomes a home to any of the farmworkers?

A: We will, we will, it will take long long long time because if we don't see them human beings like us, they won't get this. And, for the reason, for example, right now I can see families that have spend many years here separated because the man is working in another state and the woman is here. They don't have food, they don't have to pay their bills, they don't have facilities to move. They don't have and I ask them why don't you have right now all that you should have to pay your bills. They say "because my husband is working, trying to work in another state and the work there is going very slow" and this happen and these families will suffer very much and according to these families the ag salaries are very small salaries. They have a hope, the hope that the children that they will grow and they will continue studying and maybe they will come the professional in the future. The hope of this family is not what I can do for them, because I can do only a little for them, the government, they won't do for them all that they are supposed to do to give them a higher style of life. The only hope that this family have in all farmworker type that live here the only hope that they have is the children. For the reason, we need to work with the children. We need to give them all that we can. Especially saying them "what are the mistakes that our youth are doing and why are they doing this and what they are supposed to be doing for success." And they, I feel very sorry when I know that at the schools we can find groups that are a real danger for these children. Because we can have at the schools, at the schools, there are gangs. And these gangs operate, they have actions, and the school doesn't do any to stop this. And they know that they, when we have for example, a migrant child that goes to the school, and they go for example to sixth or seventh grade, and they say they receive a message from this group that says "you must be integrated with us" "you must wear special dress. You must do all this. If no, be careful because we will make you, daño. Te vamos a lastimar. We will hit you, yeah." And this happen in the school. We have at the school, eh, children that say to another children "do you have a do you have a girlfriend? Do you have girlfriend? If you don't have girlfriend you are…..You must have a girlfriend." And for the reason we can see children making mistake because they are supposed to only to study, to get degree, and then you can think like a man like a woman but no like a children. For example here at the church when I have a meeting with the teenagers, and I talk with them this. Your girlfriend, if you are men, your girlfriend is your books, your studies. And at the girls "your boyfriend is your books, your studies" when you have a title, a degree, you can think in this. But right now you make mistakes. The most important is take care of our adolescents who are teenagers and provide them all that we are supposed to give them to be success. Study, study, study. No girlfriend, no boyfriend. Friends only, without compromise. Because girl and boyfriend is a very high word.

Q: So you were talking about the government earlier with Obama being elected as president do you think that anything is going to change that will help the farmworkers' situation?

A: I don't know. I don't think because right now we are in recession. The country has big big economics and social problems. And they will work with this. Right now for example we have the immigrant problem, problem that we have now. More than twelve million undocumented people here. And according with the new government, we won't have a real hope to resolve this problem, to solve this. Everybody ask "would this presidential do something to fix this problem?" nobody knows, nobody can give an answer and for the reason I suppose if they don't take care of a real real problem that the united states has this problem no for the undocumented people the government has this problem for the same government that let accommodate in jobs, in institutions, 12 million or 13 millions of people. They let, accommodating. And we are supposed to have laws. But we didn't enforce. No "do, do, you are undocumented." And the government knows that we are full of undocumented people and right now they say "no all these people must go back to their countries." Why you let them to install? Why? No, they solve this problem. How? All they are needing to be legally here and enforce the laws. After this, nobody can give job to undocumented people. I agree. And I think that this government won't do any for the farmworkers.

Q: Well how do you feel that the local, like the North Carolina, how do you feel that the political atmosphere is towards farmworkers?

A: Don't take care. When I know that the, I knew, that in north Carolina there are three inspectors for all camps in north Carolina. I ask myself, "what could be better for the farmworkers?" only three inspectors for thousands of camps, I don't know how I can see in a camp where the place was inspected because when I go to the camps I can see that the place was inspected. And I can see in these conditions and all that this place has to be accepted to keep farmworkers there. I don't know how. If we have three inspectors for all camps, if we have not enforcement of the laws to keep the lives of the farmworkers, if we can not see any requirements for the growers, to take care of the farmworkers, if we don't see any, any, any, the government doesn't do what it's supposed to do. And you, and I, I can not be an activist. Why? Because as an activist I can make noise. I can make noise, yell, cry, noise. We need to reach, like I told you before, people with power. The churches, the government, by friendship, by something. To help, reach these people, and these people will make the enforcement of the laws. And we will see changes in camps.

Q: How, what's the role of this agency in making, helping North Carolina become more of a home for farmworkers?

A: When the farmworkers come, they understand that the CMFF is part is part of their home. Because when they come in they are accepted, they are very welcome, and they feel like a family, like a home. They feel here that they have some of his home. Because they, if they have some problem, we try to give them our support to solve this problem. If they have questions, we try to give them answers. If they have needs, we try to fill them and all all all we love. Because we won't ask for any from them. No. your presence is the most important here. And, you say, la palabra, how do you define home. I define that yes, CMFF, is a home for the farmworkers. And I feel. I have see this, because the farmworkers they call me from mexico and they say "oh, thank you thank you" they say to me "I explain people in my country what this CMFF does for us and they can not believe us" and I think that the CMFF is a unique program in the United States. I receive four years ago a visit from a very important person from NY. When he came he knew the programs and we talk about CMFF. He said "it's impossible to believe that the ___ church can have this ministry here in north caorlina" maybe could be have this ministry in new jersey, Pennsylvania, but north Carolina? And I feel very proud of this priveledge to work in this ministry because we, we don't ask "help, help, help" no. the ___ church, not in NC the diosisis, they are spending and giving support to this wonderful program. Millions and millions of members of the church help here because this is a project. And my vision is this, that we have in the program, this program is our visitor, guest, and I have seen over the year many visitors. Sometimes they send students from UNC, they come here for one week, some we have seen a visit from a school of 60 people and they spend 2 weeks here. And we have received many visitors. We came one week, and I try to give them a special feeling when they come here because I told them "this is the CMFF but if you want this one will be your ministry" because you can help. How? We have many programs. You can help us, we won't ask you for money, money, no. we know that money is very important to develop program, maybe you can not be part of a special program like food, like clothing, like ESL, like adopt a camp, Christmas gift, easter basket, and many program that we have. You can give us monetary support. And I hope that this ministry won't stop. This ministry will continue growing, growing, growing. And I am very happy when I see hundred of boys and girls that come here because this is the hope that we have. If we have visitors, if we have you here visiting this ministry will continue giving hope to continue success in NC. And for the reason I can say you, Koehler, I can say you this is your ministry, your ministry. Keep us in your mind.

Fito/Arturo Interview

(Q:Koehler Briceño, E: Elias, A: Arturo, F:Fito) 1/31/08

I drove with Elias to a FW camp outside of a NC city down a two-lane highway. We passed by houses on both sides, one yard had a horse in it, and a couple of churches. There were three gas stations/quickie marts along the highway over the entire 45 minute stretch, one was Spanish (Doña Maria). We turned off of the highway onto a dirt road, passed by a house, and continued through a tree line into a clearing with fields, a (plant) nursery, barn/garage, and 4 trailors scattered amongst the dusty landscape. Three of the trailors were deserted, waiting for the harvest season to be filled with farmworkers. Elias commented that the season before, about 100 farmworkers had shared three single trailors. After the interview, we walked around inside of them. On one of the ends, there was a room with two steel-framed beds and 5 rusty-colored-stained mattresses piled on top. I asked if there was a mattress for every farmworker, and Elias replied that, no, they often push the mattress together and sleep in rows. There was a small bathroom with a toilet and sink, and another bedroom on the opposite end (in between was just an unfurnished, open, area. According to one of the farmworkers that I interviewed with (A: Arturo, F: Fito), two families had shared that room. In less space than a third of a single trailor, two families with at least 6 kids between them had resided for the North Carolina summer. The trailors had cement blocks piled up to serve as steps up to the door. Along the outside of one trailor were two "new" showers, one for women and one for men, that had plywood doors and enough room to stand straight up in.

Chickens, cats, and a pig (tied to a tree), all personal property of the Farmworkers that I interviewed, lounged around the yard outside Arturo's family trailer, another single, that also had a platform that served as a front porch. The two farmworkers were isolated. Their decision to stay in NC and work during the off season was a result of their families, not wanting to drift around the states, but the tradeoff for staying with one's immediate family was to lose touch with friends and fellow workers who followed the harvest down south to Florida.

An interesting comparison between H-2A and undocumented worker camps, revolves around the female presence. There are hardly any (if at all) female workers who come through H-2A because the grower is able to specify the type of worker that he prefers (I doubt that there has been less laborers offered/present/willing to work than needed, but I can mention this in interviews with the growers). Many times, the FW who come through H-2A will have to pay for at least one way of their trip to/from NC (they will start work owing the grower a certain amount for "travel fees"). Although undocumented workers are also obligated to find money to pay for their trip to the USA, they do not leave once they get here, and therefore in the long run it is cheaper. Also, undocumented workers have higher likelihoods of being recruited in groups from their hometowns, and therefore bringing the same community with them to the USA that they had in their country of origin. Further, there are a higher percentage of female undocumented workers who are present in the camps. Fito actually met his wife in the USA because they were both undocumented agricultural workers. Undocumented camps have a larger family aspect to them, whether it is actual families living there, or groups of workers who are all from the same area, which creates allegiances and bonds if they were not there already. This also, however, makes it less important to interact with FW from other countries; I do not know if this is as prevalent in H-2A camps. One example of this hometown comraderie, is the relationship between Elias and Fito. Elias is the godfather of the eldest of Fito's three children (all three are elementary aged or younger), and they are both from the same town in Mexico. Elias' father recruited Fito to come work in the USA through him (he "sponsors" groups of workers and finds them work with growers in NC, he serves as the middle man and ensures them work, food, lodgings, etc). People from the same hometown "look after each other." Additionally, when I asked Fito if he had ever considered working through the H-2A program, he replied that this option was not publicized in his home town, and that coming to the USA with a contractor was the only way that he was aware of.

We interviewed in Fitos' family's trailor, which was the first one that you see as you drive into the "camp." It is located right next to the blueberry nursery. We sat on two couches covered in brightly-colored blankets, across the room from each other. In the far corner was a small, 15" tv. One of his kids was hiding from me between the couch and trailer wall when I walked in, and then giggled when I "found him" and scampered into through the kitchen into the closed off room, where he stayed with him mom and two other siblings during the entire interview. The microphone picked up their giggles and shrieks more clearly than anything else. Arturo and Fito were shy, inclined to one-line answers unless Elias encouraged them to give specific examples. Arturo was very emphatic about answering questions concerning the grower and work. He always had positive answers, never indicated any specific troubles or problems with his life in NC. Fito responded to the majority of the questions, was very centered on his family (he smiled and even laughed when referencing his children and wife, as well as his own childhood). Both farmworkers turned to Elias for reinterpretations of the questions or elaboration.

Q: Qué significa para usted la palabra hogar? (Lugar, espacio, sentimiento, cuál tipo de ambiente, sentido, personas, etc.)

F: de hogar? Um. Depende es muy profundo. De hecho que tiene más…

E: La palabra qué significa "hogar" para ustedes

A: Son hogar familia,

E: Qué significa hogar para usted. hogar

F: Con la familia, los hijos, el trabajo. Um. Cuando uno vive bien. Cuando todos estamos bien. Que no le falta para comer. Y, pos, un pocito de trabajo para ir, sacando para ir comiendo.

Q: Cuando alguien dice "hogar," ¿tiene una imagen, algún sentimiento, algún olor, u otra cosa específica en que piensa Usted?

F: Ah, pos, en salir adelante, cuando alguien viene de México, viene con el sueño de cerrarlo, verdad, y tratar de cobrarlo

Q: Y, para usted tiene algo especifico que quiere para su hogar

F: Mm. De hecho, es lo mismo. (SILENCE SILENCE SILENCE)

A: Falda. Falta de (y?) llevar bien

F:sí.

A: Pues, decir, más que luchar, sigue luchando, trabajando. Con poco con mucho, pos, salir adelante. Más que nada, como se dice, pos precisamente, más que haya trabajo, para sobresalir, para vivir. Y, pos, lo unico que uno que pide, que haya trabajo.

Q: ¿Dónde está su hogar? ¿Por qué?

F: Aquí.

E: Meaning…where they´re from, from Mexico?

Q: No, donde está su hogar.

E: Dónde se consideras tu hogar

Q: mm-hmm

F: Pos, venimos de méxico.

E: Y, quiere que considera su hogar ahora (Elias is trying to interpret questions that I read to them as I go so that they can understand them, interpret them, answer them better. There is some side commentary between them many times, with just Elias elaborating on what, specifically, the question is). Que están aquí. O se sienten más que su casa, allá o aquí.

Q: O puede ser los dos

F: Aquí.

Q: Cree que se puede tener más de un hogar?

F: pues, yo pienso que, echandole ganas sí.

Q: ¿Cree usted que Carolina del Norte será su hogar? ¿Por qué si o por qué no?

E: cree usted que viniendo a carolina del norte ya viene su donde usted considera su hogar. Y si es así compara lo que ustedes, porqué, cuál es la diferencia

F: Sí. O sea aquí. Aquí porque, por, sabes que aquí tenemos un pocito más tiempo. Y, pos, las cosas son más…hay más ayudas aquí. Para la familia.

Q: Qué tiene que pasar para que Carolina del Norte sea su hogar? Dijo que ayudas, más ayudas para la familia?

F: uh huh

Q: ah huh, y que, está con su familia y por eso es su hogar?

F: ah huh

Q: um, ¿Cree usted que siente una conexión más fuerte con Carolina del Norte, específicamente, o con los Estados Unidos en total? ¿Por qué?

F: Aquí donde estemos o en Florida (confusion, look at Elias for reference)

E:ustedes sienten que donde viven que hay más ayudas aquí en carolina del norte que en los estados como florida. Se sienten que hay más apoyo, se sienten más seguro (sí) aquí en carolina del norte que en otros estados y por qué

F: que aquí hay más ayuda

E: ayuda en qué

F: o sea, en los niños, todo eso

Q: y, encuentra que hay más ayuda aquí en carolina del norte que en todo el resto de los estados unidos, para usted?

F: Bueno, pos, nada más, porqué e he estado más (en carolina del norte) y por los más estados no sé o sea cuando que mira, yo siento que lo mejor aquí.

Q: Y, desde cuándo ha trabajado usted aquí en los Estados Unidos

E: Que, tanto tiempo tiene aquí trabajando en los EEUU

F: como nueve años

Q: y ¿Por qué quería trabajar aquí?

F: Pues, ahorita porque pos allí no hay casi trabajo y andar por arriba y por abajo pos como que no conviene, no sale. Y, más con la familia. Y pos aunque sea allá pocita pero como quieras llevando no hay

Q: Y, al principio cuando vino a los EEUU para trabajar al principio su familia podía venir con usted.

(CHILDREN LAUGHING AND PLAYING IN BACK ROOM WITH MOM, about 2 years)

F: no, no, no había familia

Q: y, desde cuándo ha estado con su familia?

F: tiene como seis años. Somos seis años.

Q: mm-hmm, y porqué podía venir también?

F: No, ella pos se vino de allá y aquí la conocí.

Q: mm-hmm. Oh, sí?

F: sí

Q: ohhh (laughter from him and me) um, pues, además de su familia aquí tiene más familia en Carolina del Norte o otras partes de los EEUU?

F: no, no.

Q: y, cuándo decidió vivir permanentemente en NC?

F: desde que

Q: todavía no?

F: No, es que, empezaron a venir los hijos, los niños.

Q: y, um, pues por eso, cuando termina la temporada agrícola todavía queda en NC?

F: sí

Q: y, sigue con trabajo agrícola?

F: haciendome todo un pocito

Q: sí

F: sí

Q: ¿Cuándo fue la última vez que estuvo en México?

F: como nueve años

Q: ¿Quiere regresar de visita o volver a vivir allí algún día?

F: quiero que visita algún día.

Q: sí. Algún día?

F: sí (smile)

Q: Y, todavía se siente como su hogar? Unos de sus hogares?

F: Pos, nada más que allá está familia. Qué a veces extraña. Pero, no se como confiesa acostumbro más aquí que allí.

Q: y, ¿Cuál es su recuerdo más feliz de ese lugar, allí en México?

F: Pues, cuando era niño.

Q: mm-hmm, pero tiene uno específico? (laugh) Esta bien si no

F: son muchos, muchos recuerdos.

Q: Pues, se siente bienvenido por la comunidad de NC?

F: Como dice?

Q: se siente bienvenido por la comunidad de NC

E: se sienten ustedes bienvenidos por la comunidad

F: sí

E: porqué. Como te sientes, como te recibieron la comunidad. Con toda la gente, como tú ves que se sienten bien (….)

F: reciben todos bien. Todo bien.

Q: Se siente usted parte de alguna comunidad en Carolina del Norte? Como una comunidad especifica que siente que

F: Si pos, un ejemplo, la iglesia cuando vamos. Mucha gente que……..reciben a uno bien, ehh (look at Elias)

E: Lo aceptan mucho,

A: Mucho aceptamiento, y todo reciben a la gente que llega.

Q: Y siguen ustedes las políticas de los EEUU (there was a confusion here, they thought I was asking them if they abided by the laws. They looked a little shocked, because the question was out of place in comparison to the others that I had been asking)

E: si ustedes siguen las reglas

Q: no, solamente, si, como en la televisión las políticas de Obama y, como, elecciones

E: la posición política, si esperan un cambia

A: pues, yo pienso que sí. Y espero que sí.

Q: sí, cómo cree usted que se afecta personalmente y como trabajadores las elecciones presidenciales

F: sí

E: cómo creen que se van a afectan ustedes, con uno ejemplo, vamos a tocar un ejemplo: el migatorio. Creen que paren las enredadas que la investiga, una mejor sueldo para la minorías que trabajan en los campos

A: yo pienso que sí. Esperemos que con el tiempo llega cambiar, todos los redadas que hay. Que a lo mejor, mejore aquí en los EEUU que sean las cosas un poco mejor. Eso es lo que nosotros esperemos que algún día, se puede aceptar como no entremos trabajar en los EEUU que esperemos que haya una buena repuesta.

E: Supongamos de que no vinieron los cambios que se prometieron. Entonces, que? Qué sería su método de pensar. (SILENCE SILENCE SILENCE)

A: Pos más que esperar. Sigue esperando. Es el mejor. Y sigue trabajando (smile)

Q: Siente alguna conexíon con la gente con quien trabaja? En los campos? Amistad?

F: Oh, sí, sí

Q: sí? Y dónde los conocieron, en los campos?

F: sí, en el trabajo

Q: y, ah, sigue los amistades despúes de...

F: de las, sí, por los que se quedan aquí, pos, siguen algunos amistades pero son muchos que se van por otros lados. Pues ya no.

E: los vuelven a ver el siguiente próximo año y siguen los amistades?

A: hay unos que se lleven (los amistades...?) y hay otros que ya no devolverán

F: hay algunos y otros que vienen de, de no sé pues, los de méxico se van para méxico

E: y los de san juan, y en esos familias (lists other pueblos from which workers come from in Mexico)

F: Y, y en esos. O sea aquí no pos.........se van

Q: mm hmm. Y cree que también, en los campos, existe un sentido de familia cuando todos están trabajando juntos? (I continued here because the FW looked doubtful or unsure of what I was asking them) O es más como, como una amistad?

F: Son...así, pos las amistades que conocieron...la temporada nada más (don´t last Longer)

Q: y, um, qué hacen juntos cuando no están trabajando?

F: pos, nada más allí, jugando, practicando,

Q:Y cómo es su relación con el patrón?

A: Pues, bien

Q:bien

A: sí

Q: y, cómo lo conoció

F: ummm, pos,

A: pues, así, llegando, buscando trabajo

Q: y se siente usted acogido, apreciado por el patrón

F y A: sí, sí

Q: sí? Cómo?

F: pues, por los

A: más que nada nos ha apoyado también. Con el trabajo. Y nos abre lados; con amistad y cariño, compasión. Nos apoya cuando le necesitamos, está con nosotros.

Q: Y Cree que sus intereses y situaciones son similares o diferentes que los del patrón. Intereses. Que tiene los mismos intereses. Just that, they're at the same level in where their interests lie when they are working together, in their relationship.

A: oh, sí. Pues el patron nos dice, "vamos a…quiere progresar un poquito más" y estamos (…..). Que apoyando en cualquier trabajo. Lo que quiere, quiere hace, no trabajes también.

Q: Okay, ahora, antes dijo algo sobre apoyo, que tiene en NC, pero hay algunas agencias que ofrecen más apoyo, ayuda? Para la familia, algo así?

F: o sea, pos, un ejemplo, los niños, el WIC(¿??), pues es una ayuda grande, medicaid

Q: y hay algunas organizaciones, como, dijo algo sobre la iglesia.

F: oh! Si, también la iglesia

Q: cuál iglesia?

F:La de, la pis pis, de father rafa.

E: y en que les ayuda?

F: pues, a vez que también regalan comida, así, cosas. Cómo se puede decir, ropa, y, todo eso, en las bolsitas, los med-kits. Todo eso.

Q: y, um, asistía la "Fiesta"

F: sí, sí,

Q: para cuántos años?

F: como unas, dos veces

Q: le hacen sentir bienvenido, más bienvenido, a Carolina del Norte? Las agencias, la iglesia?

F: pues, aquí hemos ido a la iglesia y nada más aquí

Q: y, solamente quedan dos más. Qué espera para su futuro?

A: Pues, que será que sean cosas buenas. Y, pues que sigue mucho trabajo

Q: Espera que algo cambie?

F: pos, esperamos que algo cambie todo eso de, como dijo en las redadas, todo eso, porque, por lo que mira este en la televisión que deportan mucha, mucha, gente y que quedan aquí los niños solos. Y pos esperamos que cambie todo eso.

Q: okay, es todo. O, so tiene algo más de decir, quiere decir.

E: ….diferentes culturas como las guatalmatecos…como comportan con ellos o sea cómo tiene una buena relación con ellos debido que son de diferentes países

A: pos, hemos compartido, un pocito de amistad con ellos trabajando. O sea, con ellos, haciendo *trabajo* y por eso preguntamos cómo está por allá en otro país, nos cuenta que es un poco más difícil, y cómo es el país por acá, por ustedes es difícil también por eso pa´acá vamos y estamos con usted. Luchando. Buscando la vida. Cuando uno, pos, se siente o se mantenga mejor, más que no.

E: Ustedes, qué piensan que todo hispano o mexicano es cierto que viene robar los trabajos de nada más de ante aquí en los EEUU cuando uno viene de mexico, es cierto o no es cierto, y porqué?

F: pos, yo pienso que no. Viene para nada más de trabajar. Viene trabajar y pues lo que lo único que viene.

89

A: O sea, pues, yo que que no que eso no es cierto. Por todo el trabajo en el campo lo hacemos todos que venimos de mexico y de otras países, o sea los del campo.

Q: mm-hmm. Pero, quieren que sus hijos hagan, trabajen en los campos también? Qué quieren para sus hijos?

F: pues, tiene que aprender de todo un pocito

Q: pero para su futuro, qué quieres?

F: No, que estudien, que le echen ganas. Pero también que aprender un pocito del campo.

Q: sí

F: mm-hmm.

E: que no se pierden las raíces.

F: sí

E: este. Ahora los diferentes cuestiones del campo…especialmente con las mujeres, habían la cuestión de los embarazos por la cuestión de las pesticidas. Ahh, como vemos. Ustedes qué opinan de eso, crean que deberían tener los patrones mejorar de esto o que hay una ley sobre esto para que no salgan niños afectados. Especialmente los que estamos aquí en el campo, que estamos expuestos a pesticidas y toxicados y todo eso, qué opinan de esto?

A: pues, que deben tener un poco…cuidado. O más que nada también que no se meten las lineas o que no se permiten las mujeres así que sean embarazadas.

F: que no se meten allí dentro donde hay químicos.

Q: por eso sienten que las leyendas de NC sobre los pesticidios se pretejen, que deben, ah, ser más estrictos.

E: creen ustedes que deben ser más estrictas sobre ese punto?

F: sí.

Q: Pues, a veces todavía siente que tiene que trabajar en los campos cuando todavía hay pesticidios?

A: O, nono, cuando hay pesticidios?

Q: sí

A: pues hay nada más que no se meten la gente, verdad. No se permiten.

E: la pregunta fue que a veces han o ustedes han tocado las plantas donde había todavía el olor

F: no

A: no, no ha pasado nada de eso.

F: cuando ya ha pasado todavía.

A: cuando esprayan las cosas, las plantas, o todo de eso, se toma descanso.

Q: y, por todo el año ustedes están con el mismo patrón? o cambian?

F: ah, cuando empiece la blueberry estamos, o sea, estamos en diferentes partes. Con la blueberry, tabaco, camote,

Q: pues con diferentes

F: sí patrones

Q: yeah. Okay.

E: y la cosa de sus alimentos, he visto que su lancherito……entonces tienen ustedes la oportunidad de alimentarse bien bien que no son todos desmejorados con los hijos que van a enfermar

F: pos, hay muchos que no. Muchos que pos con una comidita ligerita. Yo he visto unas papitas no más.

E: muchas marruches (laughter everywhere, meaning that lots of people survive off of cheap noodles)

A: y otra que, por, será que vienen ya cuando o salen cansados y ya por no preparar algo, pos nada más que una huevito, una marruche.

E: ahora nos dice que…conversación con mucha gente de diferentes orígenes. Y piensan que nosotros con malos, unos borrachos. Que buscamos dinero y ganamos pero no poner atención a la familia. Es cierto?

F: umm, pos, con los que nosotros, que han vivido, sí toman su cerveza el domingo. Y, pero, así que no hemos visto así que se. Pero unos cuenten que sí. Pos entre los. Los mismos que nos juntamos, platican.

E: pero ese viene de la raíz que por la misma que están solos, extrañando la familia, pos en una manera para poder relajarse o calmarse o creen que es para adicción?

A: pos, uno debe así cuando se sienten solos.

F: se acuerdan de todo la familia

A: y hay otros que sí, pos, unos que sí.

E: y los hispanos, los del campo, tienen aquí el imagen de drogadictos, que piensan ustedes de eso?

A: creo que no es cierto. Pos yo creo que los hispano, no. No vienen a robar. Viene a trabajar. Y pos, para mí, no creo eso.

E: y en la cuestión de las drogas?

A: pos, en cuestion de las drogas, pienso que hay algunas personas que le gustan y algunas que no. pocito de todo.

E: nosotros los campesinos ganamos…muy poco. Por eso dicen que las mujeres de mexico tienen que ser prostitutas. Es cierto?

F. si he oido mucha de esto per no he visto nunca de esto, nunca. No sé si es cierto pero sí se habla. Sí han oído.

E: y en la cuestión del tráfico de gente. Exista en el día de hoy o ya no? (asking questions about people being paid to bring over laborers, kind of along the lines of a slave trade)

A: no pienso que ya, ya, casi ya no. Ya no porqué había mucha gente aquí que venía así pero no se mire ya.

F: cuando nosotros nos venimos, venimos solos. O sea con otro que ya conocía. Pero el Luciano no traía gente sino que había algunos que ya han viajado solos. Y Vicente traía algunos dos nada más, para compañeros. Y así nos venimos nosotros. Éramos cuatro nada más cuando venimos. Nos cobramos como cien dólares nada más. Por desierto (they crossed the border over the desert with a guide that charged them about 100 dollars)

Q:Y nunca quería hacer el H-2A?

E: Ustedes nunca querían pasar con contratados?

F: pues, no porque en eso tiempo, pues, allí casi no escuchaban nada de eso. O sea que venía gente con contratada. Y pos ya está cuando hemos escuchado algo ya estamos aquí. Pero ya cuando venimos ya no estaba eso en mexico.

E: cuánto se cobraban?

A: en aquel tiempo cobraban ochocientos. Para eso tiempo ya.

BREAK IN THE INTERVIEW UNTIL ELIAS HAD SOME MORE QUESTIONS

E: Los del campo, nos consideran…drogadictos, que piensan ustedes sobre eso?

A: que no

E: porque no?

A: porque los hispanos, no. No vienen a robar, vienen a trabajar.

F: Y, pos, para mi, no creo eso.

E: y de la cuestión de las drogas?

A: cuestión de las drogas? Creo que hay personas que le gustan y personas que no. Como todos, o sea, un pocito de todo.

E:..Bueno, dos preguntas más y después nos relajemos. Uno que es muy delicado tocar, pero es de la cuestión de que nosotros como campesinos ganamos…muy poco. Pa'seguir adelante pero, se dicen que ha traído que las mujeres de México, Guatemala, Chiapas, Veracruz, donde sea, pasan….prostituirse. Es cierto eso…o eso no es cierto?

A: Pos, si es cierto, he oído mucho de esto pero nunca hemos visto eso. No hemos visto, o sea…pero sí ha oído comentarios sobre eso, sí han oído.

E: Y a la cuestión de todavía hay trafico de gente que existe hasta el día de hoy o ya no.

F: Pos, yo pienso que ya, ya, ya casi, ya no. Ya no. Porque sé que había, había mucha gente aquí que venía así y ya casi no se miren. Ya habían, han parado con eso, ya.

E: Y de los conocidos, saben cuantos cobraron…y las reglas que tenían?

A: Pos, para nosotros nos venimos, nos venimos solos. o sea con otros que ya conocían…ya sabían y ya…no traían gente. Sino que cada persona que venía, venía solo. Y siempre cuando se venían y se traían algunos dos, nada más. Y así nos venimos nosotros. Eramos cuatro, nada más, cuando venimos. Y cobrábamos cien dolares, nada más.

F: Es cierto, nada más.

Q: Y nunca quería hacer, como, H-2A?

E: Que nunca quisieran ustedes pasar como contratados?

F: Pos, no porque en ese tiempo cuando ya…casi no se ha escuchado de eso, o sea que venía gente contratado.

A: Y, pos, ya está cuando hemos escuchado ya estábamos aquí.

Q: mm-hmm

F: y, pos, cuando venimos ya, ya no había eso en México

E: (SOME QUESTION ABOUT WHEN THEY CAME HOW MUCH THEY WERE CHARGED TO BE BROUGHT ACROSS THE BORDER)

A: en aquel tiempo, nos cobraban algunos ochocientos…Para ese tiempo ya.

E: Y pagaban controlado o tenían alguien aquí que les pagaban y todo eso.

A: Unos, unos…tenían así conocidos, y esos, pos, ya los pagaban allí. O otros decian que, con trabajo.

E: decían..la vida de campesino..que viven mucha gente…como sardinas. Cómo es la vida allí, o cómo es…que respeten sus cosas.

A: pos, se buscan unos sí…entre los que ya conocen, o entre amigos. O a veces que, o andan unos dos, tres, cuatro. A pos ya le dicen al patrón que estamos juntos, queremos estar juntos y pos, así, así es para cada uno. Buscan las personas que..con los amigos, con quien tienes más confianza.

Q: mm-hmm

A: Y así son los demás. Ellos también buscan sus, se buscan entre ellos amigos. Ya, es bueno así en los cuartitos.

E: y a la cuestión de las parejas, como se hacen las parejas?

F: Pos, les dan allí su cuartito…en una parte

E: y los que tienen familia, tienen niños

F: Pos, se traen alli. Pos allí…comparten espacio en su cuartito alli.

E: con todos los niños

F: con los niños

E: y la cuestión de la escuela para los niños . cómo las…el patrón…

F: hay unos que estaban, chiquititos, y…con la señora

Q: Y conocía a su esposa porque ella trabajaba en los campos?

F: um, ella trabajó alli…un, un tiempo así nada más, y conocíamos

Elias Interview

Q: How do you define "home"?

A: Home, well, home to me, let's see, it depends I guess. The definition of home. To me home, it's the place where I can go and rest, lay down, relax, forget about the world outside and be with the family, leave the problems that I've been facing day by day, the challenges outside the door. Spend quality time with the family and enjoy, especially with the kids. And, uh, not bringing home any problem or issue into the house. My house is like my sanctuary my shelter where I can just relax and be myself.

Q: When someone says "home" is there a specific image, emotion, smell, or anything else that comes to mind?

A: (laugh), yes yes yes, well by the time I open the front door or back door the smell that comes to me are the tortillas, nice homemade tortillas or the nice, uh, cooking, the rice the beans, noises of all the kids running to the door, greeting me, and hoping to see if I brought some candy or toys. And they be competing against each other to see which I pay attention to, tell me what they did in school, how they behaved, if the granddaddy, grandmamma spank them or not spank them. at the same time they tell me we want you to sit with us, watch cartoons with us, play computer game with us. which the first thing I do is check up on homework. Uh the other thing is, that I do them a bedtime story. I make a story up based on what I've been going through daily. That day and just put characters to make up a sotry, which they really love. And I just like, really the nice smell when I give momma and daddy a hug. Then I feel, you know, safe.

Q: Can a person have more than one home?

A: Yes. Why? Because, in my case, I'm a migrant person, came from a migrant family, consider myself to be a migrant person. So, when I am here in NC and I get a house, but I also have another house in the state of florida and when I was younger we used to travel in different states and even though they were labor camps back then they were still considered to be my home. Even though I was in school and in the weekends I was in the fields or the days off when there was no school I was in the fields I was sleeping, too, at a labor camp. In that little 16 by 16 space to be my room, my special place, my home, my shelter. And, the workers that I share in the labor camp I see them and they see me as one of their own, family. Take care of each other and look after each other. And I share emotional feelings, we learn how to become adults or we learn how to live in another world where we are misunderstood but we have to, people will just have to look at us to understand us and live what we live through and go what we go through so they can be able to understand us.

A: Again, when they say home, I really don't feel like I really have a home because of the way things are right now. As we speak today, right now in the place that I'm living, yes, I own it but whenever I'm not around or pass away, the lord takes me, that home ain't gonna be my home again, it belongs to the government again. I don't have a home, actually. I travel a lot. Momma and daddy always told me that the best home you got is the outside world. Your blanket is the sky, your lights are the stars, and, uh, again we are just farmworkers we are raised to adapt to the outside world.

Q: So, so said that you don't feel as if you have a home.

A: No

Q: What has to happen in order for NC to be your home?

A: Change. Like change in all major factors, like for example the law, change with the discrimination that's been going on, change with the racial, change with the system, change with the government, change with the senators, talked about us, mistreat us. A change where we can actually be treated as human beings, not some type of animal.

Q: Is there a difference between a place that *is* your home and a place that *feels* like home? What are the differences?

A: It, it is. Just to give a few examples. It can also, when I was younger we were in California, sacramento California, and everybody knows that California right now is populated by a whole bunch of Hispanics. And believe it or not over there there is more, more rights, where you be treated equally. More help, help, especially with health issues, for migrant, a lot of migrant families, the law will be fair, and you be treated as what you really supposed to be treated. They don't ask you if you're legal or not legal when they pull you over (287G NC). On the contrary they ask for your ID, driver's license, um. It's fair, it's fair up there. But once you go to different states, here up north it's much different. They call you an "alien." Which you're not really an alien, you're just another person with different ethnic background.

Q: So you think that California having equal rights contributes to it feeling like a home?

A: Yes. California, Texas, and even Florida. Even Florida.

Q: Do you think that you feel a stronger connection to NC or the USA?

A: No I don't feel that connection, on the contrary I feel more challenging. I feel it's uh it's a challenge that you will learn that the true meaning the true definition of "only the stronger will survive" and what I mean by that is because if you're trying to move one step forward in what you're trying to achieve in your goals in your dreams it's a challenge because there's always an obstacle. But at the same time, make sure you're always being a grownup person, at the same time, and be more cautious. And at the same time make sure you vale what you really want to be, who you want to be. Make sure you really pursue that happiness. And at the same time, they may tell you it's not easy to accomplish what you're really trying to do. But with you do you can really taste it and say "wow I finally did, I did manage to accomplish." So, to me NC is a really challenging state.

1. So, with the work that you do, with each challenge you meet are you working towards it, making it your home, or are you just working towards making it more fair?
    a. To me, through my eyes, I'm working to trying to make a difference. Trying to set an example, that there are still good people. That not all people that are dressed in black are the bad guys. Um, I'm trying to make a change maybe I might be able to reach ten people out of a hundred, but I will be able to reach five and those five, as time goes on, more people will be able to understand. And may be able to follow the same steps that I am making. And that is basically what I am trying to do, I am trying to accomplish, show society that we are all are the same, brothers and sisters, just like the bible says.

Q: How did you come to the United States?

A: 1986, I was six years old, papa and mama were here since 1983. And by that time, if I remember correctly, jimmy carter was the president and he managed to have the..

Q: Oh, the amnesty (Reagan was actually president, and this was the IRCA act of 86)

A: The amnesty, he accomplished it. And also, cuba had a whole bunch of pilgrims, but they cleaned their jail houses (Mariel). That was when mama and daddy got their papers and were able to bring us over. By that time in school, I was in the third grade but I had a difficult time due to the lack of language, but I still somehow managed to, uh, pass the third grade. Uh, again by signs and yes and nos. but we were taking special classes, esl classes, when I was in third grade so I learned English. So it was not really difficult. Again, thanks to that, I was able to learn English, as time went on, by listening to my friends, student friends, or my neighbors. Sharing conversation where I could practice my so-called English skills. And that really happened a whole lot more than during school and listening to the teacher.

Q: Did you come over with all of your brothers and sisters then?

A: Yes we all come at once, at one time, uh, granddaddy. Granddaddy and grandmamma were the ones that growing up, picking us up. Back then they used to live in texas, close to the border, and uh we were staying with my other grandmama and one day they just said "listen, we're gonna pick you up, so let's go" and I remember the whole trip. It was from monterrey to all the way to florida I remember it was a 12 hour drive. I remember that immigration came to talk to us to see if we knew English .but back then, granddaddy was telling us on the road what to say, so he was, my other brothers were asleep, they were younger I was the eldest one, and managed to pass through and kind of convinced me to be a chicano, a Mexican-american so I didn't have any difficulties with that, so everything ran smooth. We arrived at, I remember we left on a Saturday and we arrived Monday at 3am where momma and daddy were in florida.

Q: Have you all been back to monterrey to visit?

A: Um, well, most of all of momma's side of the family are here so...and my dad, my grandma passed away to only my granddaddy...has been staying there since he became the treasurer in that little state and after that he became the governor so he just decided to stay there and never come back (Mexico). I had planned on the year of 2004 but a lot of changed since 1986, I went back again in 2006 for two weeks to pick up my momma because she had gone to see her sister and at the same time the doctor because the doctors over there are much cheaper than over here. and then things were a whole lot different. the crime was way sky high. There are litterers almost everywhere, on the streets, moreso than there were cops, so, it was rough. There was more prostitution there were more druggies. I mean, it was bad. I thought LA was bad but, monterrey, two times worse in monterrey.

A: So, if I wanted to go back again? No. and the reason is because, everytime they see that you are from here because the way you talk and the way you dress and all the time if you are driving the police will stop you and say, hey! Uh, you're missing a tag. They come up with dumb excuses just to ask you for money. And they don't ask you for pesos, but for dollars cause they know you came from the other side. And to me that kind of hurts because you know people the ones who are over here fighting, struggling, and they're treating you different and actually, that comes to another question. You actually don't even belong over there anymore. And the reason I'm saying that because when I last, because, from then to 86 and when I went back again to the courthouse to see if my ID and social security number from up there still exist it doesn't anymore. there's nothing there. I don't have a record no more, I'm nobody up there in Mexico. I'm erased. Me and my brothers. My father. Everybody, we are all erased so we can't even vote for the next election of president up there we're just nobody (MEXICO DID NOT ADOPT THE DUAL CITIZENSHIP POSSIBILITY UNTIL ABOUT 1997). So it makes you pretty bad because over here they don't even want you even if you got your papers and you are a citizen you're still not countable.

Q: Um, so what do you think were the goals or motives of your parents to come to the USA?

A: Well like every migrant in my family, the American dream. Uh, to uh, go forward with their dreams.

Q: Did they already have family here? you said that your grandparents were in texas?

A: Yes, we've got family all over. We got family in California san diego, florida, texas, north Carolina, new york. That's all of them that I know. I know that we've got more family but I don't know them all.

Q: So did your parents meet here in the US or did they meet in mexico and then make the decision together to come?

A: They met in mexico. See here's the thing. Daddy had a good job, he graduated from the university of monterrey. He was an honor roll student. Again, back then when he was growing, his daddy was the governor, so he was a child that doesn't quite really need, you know money, anything, he was living well. But since he was the youngest child and my granddaddy, to today, he was very strict. Daddy said "well this is not for me, my ambition is something else." So he was in charge of the mexico bank, enterprise, I forget the name of it. And, uh, he was ready to get married. He met mama, I forget the story, but they met in monterrey. Mama came from, also from a good family, a wealthy family, of raising horses, agriculture. So again, her family was pretty good but, you know how it is, they didn't like papa because papa had, you know right then he was a player, he was a hound dog. But right then, mama was different so, ah, one day daddy went and decided to say "listen, I have got my older brother up there in florida and he is doing pretty well and I know that the dollar is doing stronger, two times the value of a peso over here. life over there is less stressful and better. Let me go up there with my brother and see if I can achieve and look for what I'm really looking for and pursuit of happiness." And, uh, that was in 1984 when daddy decided to go up there in florida. And he did, he stayed over there for two years with my uncle in Tampa, Florida, where they were doing citrus back then. Citrus used to be the gold mine in the whole state of florida. Since then my uncle was the, one of the biggest Hispanic famers in the citrus business.

Q: He was a grower, or a

A: A grower.

Q: So did your dad go to florida in order to work on farms or to be a grower?

A: Well, he said that he always liked to be working on a farm, which I never liked to be in the office. I was born and raised in a farm. But, uh, my granddaddy always told him that for him he was going to be a leader, a greater person. And, uh, the relationship with my granddaddy he needed to follow his steps to be more in the political instead of the agriculture business. My daddy's brother was the one that followed my grandaddy's steps, my daddy was the rebel one. So, daddy was like "no, this is not was I really like" so that's the reason he came to be a farmer. But, like everything he started from the ground. My uncle told him, "listen, here's the bucket, so you can you. You have to learn and that way you can learn how it actually works." Those two years he managed to do that and he managed to learn English and went to night schools and some community colleges in Florida. He managed to get his legal license. He managed to get a few to get workers. And in 1987 he was already a contracter. And he was being contracted by three orange growers. When that happened my uncle said "you know what the family ends here" and that was pretty bad. And the reason was because in a short time, you see my uncle, it took him twelve years to be a grower, my daddy it only took him three years to be a contracter. And a contracter until 99 daddy was a grower, a farmer, a small, little, farmer. But the thing that daddy told him was that if you're really trying to pursue something, you have to struggle, and you have to really know how to spend your money wise[ly] and sometimes you have to sacrifice and nowadays people don't do that and he said the way I learned all this is thanks to the, the way I was working at the bank. So that really taught me a lot" and he's really good with numbers, so.

Q: Are you married, do you have kids?

A: Ohh, that's very personal

Q: Sorry

A: No, that's all right, that's fine. I do have kids I got three. One of them is six, named Julian***?, the other one is five named Reuben, and my baby it's uh Johnnie, gonna be three years. No, I'm not married I'm a single dad. My kids are living with me, um. My relationship didn't really work out because when their mom, that's another story, but the thing is…she didn't like the life condition. She didn't like for me to be traveling, she didn't like for me to be helping out people. She always expected something in return. She didn't like for me to be away from the house too much, she didn't like for me to be spending time in the farm, 12 hours, and then coming home just to take a shower, sometimes I didn't eat, just to sleep, kiss my babies goodnight, pull the blankets up. And there's always something too, there were a lot of arguments, to the point that she decided to leave a note that said "listen I'm leaving you and the kids…" since then I've been a single dad, since 2006. So I'm playing out the role of mom and dad. Uh, in the mornings, the two older ones, they go to schools, one's in first grade the other's in kindergarten, and the baby stays with mama. And he's fixin to go to those migrant headstart, now that the season is about to start.

Q: Is that through CMFF?

A: Uh, no that's uh another one in ___ county. Since we got a blueberry farm up there they just recently open a new one. And at the same time I managed to fund money to get the school working. In the afternoon, by the time I get home, mama is the one, she takes care of them and then when I get home I pick up my, we're neighbors, I pick up my kids and bring them home, check the homework, listen to them, see what they're doing, if they've behaved. Um, purchase them any clothes if they need clothes.

Q: So, you said that, um, when you were describing home you mentioned, you talked a lot about your kids, so do you think that they're a big reason why you're why you are now more attached to NC instead of moving around as much or do you feel that you're still moving around?

A: Uh, I still, I still feel that I'm moving around. Maybe not the way my daddy and mama started, when we were young, and the reason I'm saying this is now that I've got involved and helping out so much with a lot of refugee farmworkers, minorities, small farmers, uh, migrants, from all different backgrounds. I've been flying too much to different states. And, uh, I know I don't' stay much, four days, five days max, and help out with their different problems, legal status, or they're losing land, can't get a loan because they need some paperwork and I get to that, they, wherever they manage to get better, a loan to purchase that small little acreage, they're trying to take the land away, that's where I come in. I've been called the, in Spanish it's "el abogado de los pobres" in English it's "the lawyer of the poor" but my flight ticket they all come from my own expenses. And they're just people I meet in different conferences, reunions, that I get invited. So I give them my card, they just call me and I'm "well yeah, I got time" and I swing by there. And I don't expect nothing in return from them. and I guess that was one reason that my baby's mama got mad. Because she says " nobody's helping you when you in times of need and you're helping them and I don't see none of them giving you a hand." And it's not some much about what you're expecting back but it's about how much you're giving back and again that's a different, that's another story and I'll be more than happy to explain why (NOTES ABOUT BROTHER).

Q: Which three things have to be present in a place in order to designate it as your home?

A: Well, in my own personal view, first it would be that we get equal justice. Second, that, uh, the health issue, that we all get the help for people. And third, if those two things we have manages to get accomplished, then I would feel really, really…good…and I would feel that I am really now at home.

Q: Do you feel welcome in North Carolina?

A: Hypocrite way, yes. Honestly, no. and the reason I'm saying hypocrite way is, people will give you a handshake or a palm on the back just because they know how much you are worth but if you don't have that much…money signs, and you're here they won't even shake your hand, and at the same time make you feel pretty bad.

Q: What needs to change in order to make you feel more welcome?

A: What needs to change. Well, again, those two things.

Q: Do you feel like part of any specific communities in North Carolina?

A: What do you mean? Explain yourself.

Q: Like they can be different, if you participate in a football league, or if you go to the church services or, even the organizations you participate in. Just, different communities, like when you were talking, when we were having our interviews with the farmworkers you were talking about how sometimes people from the pueblos back home, how they form their own communities in NC as well instead of...

A: Well, let me see if I understood you right. Um, in the community, I do feel welcomed a lot, uh,

Q: Which communities?

A: Two communities, the Hispanics and the African American community. And up more, like in Pittsboro, I've felt really welcomed by the Hmong community

Q: So all minorities. So, you don't, this is a little off topic, you don't feel as if when people classify everyone as latinos or Hispanics it's kind of like putting on a label that isn't, like, you all come from different places and different cultures, so you don't find it offensive when they do that?

A: Um. I do sometimes, and I'm going to explain to you why. First of all, when they say latinos and Hispanics, they need to understand the definition of latinos and Hispanics. Latinos and Hispanics. Latinos are Puerto Ricans, from Honduras, el Salvador, Cubans, and from Dominican republic. That's latinos right there. And they're, thanks to what they do, especially with the stealing jobs, and what I mean by that, going to factories, construction, uh working in carpenting work, even working on fast food restaurants. We get blamed that we're the ones stealing their jobs. The definition for Hispanics are people that come up from mexico, in all different states of mexico. And the Hispanics that you are going to see working in the fields, working in packing houses, working in chicken houses and turkey houses. That's about it. And we're always the ones being chased around, on the borders, and being shot in the head. We're the ones trying to make a difference. But, thanks to the confusion of the Latinos, we're also being blamed for what they do on top of…being blamed for being a terrorist just for coming to the USA.

Q: So

A: So, yes I do get a little offended. Sometimes I'm like "wait a minute you have to define me" trying to explain that either Latino, this is what Latino does, and Hispanic is different, this is what we do.

Q: How did you come up with these definitions for Latino and Hispanic?

A: Every Hispanic and every latino knows this. I have met no latino and no Hispanic that doesn't know it the same what that I am describing it to you. Uh, that's where people will come, being ashamed saying "oh, no, no, I am not Hispanic, I am Latino" and you tell them "well, why are you saying you're Latino" and they'll tell you "oh, I come, I do this, I'm not the one being on the field, I'm not the mule, the working mule, I'm not the one going to be paid the low wages"

Q: So you think these definitions come up according to what sort of job they perform?

A: Oh yes. And you're missing one more here which is very important. Chicano. Chicano is way different from those two. And Chicanos don't like Hispanics.

Q: Yeah. So. Um, I had a conversation, I work in a restaurant, and some of the kitchen staff, a lot of them are from, um, Venezuela and there is one Mexican worker and he was saying that there are chicanos in North Carolina. And before I only thought that they were in California or in the western part of the USA and that it was kind of their own grouping of, kind of like the first generation of

A: Mexican Americans

Q: Yeah, Mexican Americans

A: Well, to give you an example, my three kids? My three kids, even though I am originally from mexico, my three kids they're already chicanos. So any Hispanic that have kids they're already chicanos. Latinos, they have a different name that I can't remember, the name they give their kids, but it's not chicanos. Chicano, they just don't like Hispanics, and if you look on the immigration status, all the immigration patrol officers, all of them are chicanos. There's not a single white male. Or black male.

Q: So you think that, um, Hispanic, it's not necessarily from mexico but people who work in the fields? Because there are some people from Honduras that work in fields too

A: People that are working on, there are, don't get me wrong, but see, again, this is where we are getting ourselves more into specific detail, people that work come over from Honduras, people from Honduras, right now, from el Salvador, from Columbia, they're refugees that are running from all the situations going on in their countries. and sometimes they're refugees, so they can get paperwork, but they can still bring them over here because of their situation. So what they do, they know they can't get a job like the rest of the latinos do, so the only option they got is to go to the fields. You see most of those guys, when they go to the fields, the guys they normally have the prostitution business going on, they're the guys that have the connections with the coyotes, they're the guys that normally dealing with the drugs inside labor camps, or the alcohol. Then again, there's always good and bad guys. Again, I've been since the age of six until I the age of nineteen living in labor camps and I haven't seen any different. And that's why I'm saying because I've seen it from my eyes.

Q: So you think within, like a group of undocumented workers, who are working in fields, there's definitely different kind of allegiances that form depending on where you come from?

A: Yes

Q: So, there's no real, I mean if you say a "Hispanic community," you're speaking of Mexican farmworkers but you're not talking about all of the people from latin and south America who come to the United states?

A: No. I mean I don't mind helping them if they need the help, I don't mind it at all, but the ones right now that really need the help are the farmworkers. They're the ones that we're being treating wrongfully. They're the ones that are not being paid correctly. And even though they gave the H-2A workers temporary visas, they are the slaves of this generation. Here in the state of North Carolina there has been some reports, newspapers, articles, of people that have died of dehydration of bad treatment. They don't' take them to the hospitals and that the person has passed away…me and father rafa have been dealing with this for the past three years. The farmer doesn't deal with them, they call father rafa and myself and say "hey, guess what, this guy just passed away, see if you can send him back home…" it's just bad. It's really bad. It may sound like a movie, like a movie thing, but it's not it's just the reality of life.

Q: So, can we talk about the work that you do in North Carolina? You work for your parents, who are contractors, is that right? And you also work for some aid agencies?

A: My parents, today, they're blueberry farmers and vegetable famers. But their major, major, is blueberries. Uh, in florida, they are citrus farmers. The contracting, I do it but off the side, just to find work for people who can't seem to find contractors, good people who they can trust. In fact, because, they get paid in cash but they don't get paid what they really work for because the contractor will say "well listen, just for taking you to that farm and taking you back home" and they bring a whole lot of excuses to take away money and salary. Uh, so that's why I, I mean I say "listen I will tell the farmer to pay you in check and if you have a problem to cash it, we will go to my bank and they'll cash it for you, and you don't even have to pay those two or three dollars that they charge you to turn a check into cash. That's the only guarantee I can give you if you can give me the guarantee that you can help me…pick up the produce from that farm" and it has worked out pretty well. Again I don't do it to get rich or anything, again, just to help out and kill some time. Blueberries it takes three years to get your production back and on the fourth year you get your money back. You've got a lapse of time, and I don't like being at the house.

Q: Do you also work with Father Rafa?

A: With Father Rafa I do work a lot, ever since 1999. And I've been with him going to labor amps. To H-2A labor camps, especially, to see what is the needs that they need, the help they need, how they've been treated, if they have any concerns with the grower, with the farmer. We have also seen other labor camps that are being, migrant workers, or season workers have been staying, but it's a lot different. The seasonal workers have it much better than H-2A. they're more free. That they can do and go where they want to, than the H-2A workers. So our major focus is the H-2A worker. We do focus with the migrants, don't get me wrong, but we have documented and see the H-2A are really needing, are more in need of our help.

Q: So how did you get involved with CMFF?

A: Well, Father Rafa, he came one day to my labor camp…here in NC…and I was in charge of one of the labor camps, back then daddy was no longer contractor, and that was my last year of being a contractor because I decided to start being, helping daddy farming. And, uh, there was a big greyhound that came into the labor camp and nice, nine or ten brand-spanking new black vans that came. One of the guys shouted out "ah, immigration immigration" when the vans pulled in, almost in front of the door. Father Rafa came out and said "no, it's just me! I've brought some clothes and I've brought some students from chapel hill, UNC" and the vans were carrying a lot of clothing, medical supplies, even brought food, and the university students were also some members from the church. That's how I met Father Rafa. I mean, I had heard of him through mom and daddy but since, when you're in the fields, sometimes you work seven days, I wasn't able to go to church. Not that I didn't want to but the grower that I was working for was way behind and he couldn't wait. And we talked, shared our ideas, and I told him what was going on, and I was more than happy to help him out not charging, not looking for any money from the church or anything. From there on we build a good relationship and as time went on and weeks went on and months went on and years went on we became carrots and peas. But, uh, he's been sending me to churches to speak to ask for help, not money help, but to bring people to the labor camps and see if they can adopt labor camps so that way they can build a good relationship with farmworkers so they can know that beyond the jar we've got people that are living in bad conditions and they need help like used clothes, or a used fan, or a refrigerator or stove. Or just, just companionship so they won't feel isolated. Which is the big word that we use is isolation.

Q: So, do you have an official position there?

A: Um, in 2007, uh, father rafa came up to me and said "listen, we have, the board of the CMFF church have decided to ask you to be a member; our first, young, migrant-working member of the whole north and eastside dioceses of North Carolina." So, I was taken aback, I said yes! Yes, I will. Yes, I will. But then I'm like wait, I don't have to be preaching or sharing the bible or all that. So he laughed and said "with you, since you're living in two worlds, the American world and the farmworker world we can have a better understanding and connection to bring and helping out the people. And you'll be able to go [to] places that I cannot be able to go." And so I said, yes, you can count me in. And since then I have been the youngest one member and the only Hispanic member to be in the board.

Q: So, Father Rafa is not a member of the board?

A: Not a member, but, he still puts his two cents and, you know, but he's not a person to vote on something, to say "let's vote or not vote on this."

Q: So what does the board, what is the, just, main goal of the board?

A: The main goal of the board is to get as many churches from different religions, to get them involved in helping out the farmworkers because without the farmworkers there would be no food on their table. Uh, help them out, again, with clothes, canned food, medical kits, visit them. If they see that the labor camp they're living in, it's pretty bad, and if the labor department isn't doing nothing…say hey, you need to talk to this group to fix living conditions. And, uh, just to be a big family. That's the main goal and, helping out the needy. And, again, making people from different religions, churches, understanding what really farmworkers, the true really meaning of a farmworker. And the best way is not by reading books, it's you have to go and see with your own eyes. Smell, see, even taste the food because when you go up there they offer you food, and see the way they're living. People that went it really broke their hearts. And I've seen people crying, for the way that they live, it's really emotional.

Q: Um, so, you all as a board, you focus more on just helping famrowkre and just improving their conditions but you don't really get into the political side of it, and trying to

A: We, we're not trying to get into the political side for the reason that if we do, uh, we're afraid there's going to be a mixture that's no longer related to the church. They're going to seem more related, and they going to say that we're attacking actually the political system, and we don't want to go through it because then we're going to get cut off from funds, and then it's going to be, it's going to create a big chaos and we don't want that. So we're going to stay away from the political.

Q: Yeah, so you're sticking more to the humanistic, "these are people"

A: Correct, correct.

Q: Um, just, I know, with your parents as growers, and as a contractor of workers who don't come with documentation do you feel that there are conflicts between you and organizations like FWUG (Farmworker Unionizing Group)

A: Oh, heh heh heh, yes

Q: Heh, or just H-2A workers in general just about who

A: Uh, okay. The one you just mentioned, FWUG. There has been some, uh, there has been some negative issues between me and the person in charge of FWUG. There has been lots of debating on his ideas and my ideas. I'm going to explain it to you. One, his idea is trying to work with big companies where they can get people who get treated legally right, paid right, humanly right. And, but once that is accomplished, all those promises and all those letters that have been signed as petitions, all those people not one single person and there's been articles that came out last year, there has not been a single member that became member of that FWUG organization that has been really helped with all those promises that they said that they were going to help them if they sign and be supportive. None of them, til today, have been helped. And what they have done with the money they have managed to win with these big cases, with Campbells, Mount Olive the pickle, all the money FWUG has been keeping it to themselves supposedly to expand their organization to other states. But see the thing is now people from FWUG started, now I remember this because Daddy had an argument with the main fellow, and that was 1998, he met him at Nashville County, here in NC. The man was a thief. I'm sorry to say this but…people came up to him since back then and they came last year and said listen, we have covered what you told us but we have seen nothing you promised. You promised us you were gonna fix us the papers, you promised us you were going to get us a 4-1K you promised you were going to send us money, now that we're older people, to our families in Mexico. You promised you were going to help our younger people go to colleges, good schools, in California and Texas, and we haven't seen none of those. You promised you were going to help out, there were a few families who had cancer issues, and the expenses were pretty high, you promised us you could help us with that and what happened. And, uh, right now FWUG doesn't think they have the merit to say "well, listen, I don't remember you. I can't find a list that you said a certain year and certain month and certain day. So, sorry I think you're just trying to, uh, make a bad image of us by coming out here, who sent you." And, you know, kind of stuff that doesn't seem. And people have been crying to them saying "you came to my house. I signed that sheet of paper, that petition letter, you came to my house I fed you at my house and you promised me all of these wonderful things." So you're not really helping, where's the money?" Now, the man, he's driving a good car, got a helicopter.

Q: I thought FWUG, I knew they were working with big companies, but I thought they were, I thought it was just to raise the wage. Isn't that a big part, or is that

A: It is, but you have to understand one thing: Now organizations these days, it's hard to find one that you can really, really trust. Because organizations these days and especially the way the economy is, you're really finding now, who is really helping the people. Because organizations live out of other people. What I mean by that, they live out of people's fears, tears, sacrifices, grants supposedly to help out the communities.

Q: So, how do you think the CMFF is able to disconnect themselves from this, as an organization?

A: Uh, farmworker, the church, I don't consider it to be an organization and I'll tell you why. One, we're not a 501-C3, and we're not a co-op. we're just people that decided to help out the communities, from different backgrounds. We're people who decided to put our time and effort in helping out in every little situation that we possibly can. And the way we do it, it's through the riches of the relationship of the network that each individual of the board member has that has been the greatest help where we can get a lawyer we can get a doctor we can get a banker we can get, you know. With the network that each one has built up, that's the riches that the church has brought in to help out the community. So my question would be what would ever happen in the church no longer existed? What would ever happen if Father Rafa is not there? Well, it's sad to say but all that helping all that fighting that the church and Father Rafa have been doing. It would no longer be there.

Q: So, do you think, um, the Farmworker Fair that they have every year, do you think it's really important for that feeling of community between the farmworkers?

A: Yes, the Farmworker Fair, we're not doing it just to celebrate, we're doing it to make the people feel like they're in Mexico, that they're on a small rancho. Make them feel that hey, even though you're in a different country or state, here we're trying to bring a little bit back from your origin. Here, maybe it's not fancy like the way you celebrate but we're trying to bring you, all of us, to look at each other and say "hey guess what," even if you work on different farms "hey guess what I came from the same state that he came from" and building up the relationships, make them feel good. Uh, making them feel like they're really wanted. Making them, like we're thanking them for the hard labor, the sacrifice, their tears, their sweat, their humiliation. For providing that food on our table, it's just a way of saying thank you and "we see you as one of us, as family." So, every year we're trying to make a little better, for them. Because when the afternoon ends and the music stops playing and you see them getting back onto those busses or vans you see a good smile on most of all of them. You see a few tears on some of them because they wanted a nice shirt, uh, a nice something that they never thought they could get it, and it was provided to them by the church through the festival. And it's not to bring them so they can be part of the religion. Again, no, it's just a way to thank them, to make them feel welcome. That they're not alone. And the good thing, we get to eat lots of different types of food from, uh, Mexico..Monterrey, so on so on.

Q: Um, so why do you tink that NC specifically is a target state for recent immigration? And this is what, um, I've done some reading and just about how initially it was California and texas and it's shifted over to the Southeast just because of recent agricultural interest but also just because there was more labor available there compared to California where there was a lot of pre-existing, like, Chicanos or Mexican-Americans who had…

A: Well, in California, now, everything is going organic. And right now it's pretty hard to, uh, it's getting pretty hard to actually…be someone. Let me explain myself correctly. In California since the population is way too big, it's pretty hard to find a good job, even in the fields. Uh, so the reason all of us, including myself, we came to North Carolina is because NC has not been, uh, exploited. There's more opportunities for you to get more jobs in the agriculture. There's more opportunity for you to get one acre or two acre and from there you can start your own farm and call yourself a farmer. There's more opportunity that you can get from other organizations, uh, an education on how to cultivate and market your stuff. Uh, there's more opportunity compared to, again, to those states, a little bit, not too much, but opportunity on health-wise issues. That you don't get treated but at least your kids will get treated if they get sick. And, um, that's the reason we're coming over here because this is more of a country, not as much of a city, it's a city over there.

Q: So, you think, um, when people come to NC their thoughts are for their future

A: Yeah

Q: Instead of the present, like, what they work for are what their kids can get or the opportunities they see

A: Correct

Q: Down the road

A: Correct. Which parents, when they're looking for their kids just to make a better life for their child, so if they see their future, a brighter future, where they can accomplish that, in a different state, that's the person who migrates. So, basically, the kids are the ones that are going to enjoy what we are, whatever we are giving up, not us. For example if I start a farm and I am having a hard time trying to build that farm and set it up pretty good, and by the time I do it I might be already old. But my kids, they are going to be old enough to run it a lot smoother without the obstacles that I encountered. So I'll be a happy parent that I managed to accomplish that for them. that's basically what we're trying to, all migrant parents are trying to do.

Q: So, even immigrants who come here and they may not necessarily have a family or kids you think that they're, what do you think their main goal is?

A: Repeat that again please?

Q: For immigrants that come to NC to come in farms, as farmworkers, what do you think that their main goal is if they don't have kids?

A: Main goal. Well. I had that question before. And, the response that I have to that, is. If there's, if the fellow is single, he will look for himself a good wife. If the female is single, she will look for herself a good man.

Q: So they're still looking for, kind of a more permanent

A: Right

Q: Place in NC

A: Yes

Q: And do you think that you have that perspective because you work more closely with undocumented workers or do you think that H-2A workers in the long run

A: If you ask a H-2A worker how do they feel compared to an undocumented person they will say tell you that they also feel undocumented. They say that people, the reason, that so they're all stuck in it, the reason is that they're all slaves. Uh, I feel and I know this, again, because since I was six years old until the age of nineteen or twenty I have been spending most of my life: youth life, younger life, child life in labor camps and going through the same circumstance that they go through. Which, nothing has changed; history repeats itself. There's no difference.

Q: So, how do you feel that families of migrant workers have an effect on their experience in the USA?

A: The experience. Well, the way they, especially the older migrant families that I recently met up with, they have been telling me that they feel more from here than from Mexico and I'm going to say why. Because, the USA, now, and there's a time track that I think I sent to you, the USA was created by migrant people

Q: Was what?

A: Created by migrant people. That's what the word "united" stands for, and "states," because there's a lot of migrant people in different states trying to unite all these migrant people to become the united states. America became, the word of it became, after the English came and stole it from the Indians. The pilgrims, I mean, stole it from the Indians. So basically, we belong more here than anybody. Basically, without the migrants there wouldn't be any "united states." So, when I asked the older people that have been spending here most of their life, and I'm talking about people in their eighties and ninety-year-olds, we're actually, we're feeling more American than an American person does because America has been more loved by the migrant person than by the American person that lives here. We treasure America and carry America in our heart to the point that we sacrifice where we're coming from to reach America...So we feel more American even though we don't have a paper that says that. But we do feel more American, than anybody else.

Q: Um, as far as, um, people who come here to work on farms as farmworkers, do you think there is much interaction between them and then communities that are living here permanently

A: Mm, not really.

Q: So you don't think that has any influence over whether or not they want to stay, their interactions?

A: Not really and I'm, I'm, again, let's go back to question one or two: they're willing to stay if they can get some land. They can buy land, so what they can do they're looking for someone who can bring the land to them and start, you know, jump from a farmworker to a small little producer or farmer or grower. Uh, people that are staying here already, and I don't know if you've done a documentary or research, but people who are staying here already are working on keeping their houses, they prefer to stay in a stable job even though it doesn't pay them than adventuring in something else new, a new avenue. The migrant work will decide to venture and not just to see, too look how it goes, but they really have to mindset and say "well listen, I know I'm good at this because this is what I was doing back home." And so, that's what I'm saying it varies, it varies.

Q: So, you support farmworkers who decide to stay in NC and try and make it

A: I support all of them, I don't disqualify I don't disagree. Each head is a different world; the way he thinks is different so I have to be respectful of them. What I do is, "listen, this is what you want? This is what you do that will make you happy? Then let's do it" then I try and find help to help you achieve and reach that. So I don't discriminate [against any] of them, on the contrary I'm trying to listen and see how I can be a really helpful to them. and supportive at the same time.

Q: So how do you think that political circumstances in NC affect farmworkers' decision to stay here, or affect their stay in NC?

A: Yeah, it affects it a lot. When Elizabeth Dole was still running here in NC, she passed laws in Durham and Charlotte, and I think in Raleigh, and some counties, where, um, if a seasonal worker comes and rents a trailer park, house, or apartment, or just a complex, that the person who owns those buildings, will get a fine just for owning it. So what that accomplishes is many growers or farmers, American growers, they haven't been able to have good help to pick up their produce, so when that has happened, many of the farmworkers, they go instead to other states. But see those states that they've been going to, there's no jobs because the season starts in Florida, Georgia, South Carolina, NC, all those states up north, and then everything and texas. So, they're just pushing us away, and then when they see a big crowd, what happens? Then they pass another law that says "listen now that we've seen a lot of vandalism, let's get the police officers also involved so they can make the migration law" and the first thing they'll do is "hey, Hispanic, move to the side I'd like to see your papers." They don't ask you for your ID or anything so if you don't have your papers, whether you have a child or that child wasn't born here all of them get credited as delinquents. So that has really hurt us a lot, with the housing. That's the reason I'm trying to push forward more labor houses from the worker, from the grower, so it can help out not just them but also the guys or the families that have a standard home when they come from another state after they have finished the season in that state and they know they have a place to go to.

Q: Um, and then, as far as your role or, within the CMFF, do you think they play a big role in making the farmworkers feel at home

A: Yes, and, I'm going to say why. Right now we're working on a project with Design Corps; they're from Raleigh. What they do, they go out and search for grants. They're helping us with a grant to make a model fro labor housing so we can have, so we can bring growers and see the difference that with less money you can build a better house where farmworkers, seasonal workers, H-2A workers can really live on. And the best way, my mom told me "if you can make that person live in a good house, good conditions and everything that person can guarantee you more out there in the field than if you treat them in a crappy place." So we're on that, hopefully that project will be finished my this coming-up year. And you're more than welcome to take pictures if you'll be around...

A: Another way that CMFF has been working, again, through Design Corps, is a market. I don't know if you've been to the structure, they're doing a smaller flea market. Like the farmer's market but a smaller one, we're combining those two things right there at the church. The structure is there but we ran out of funds due to the fact that RMA ran out of money. RMA is an office that gets funds from Washington, you should look it up. So, we're halfway and in the market it's going to be where you can sell clothes, food, flowers, under the type of roof, we're coming up with a new solar panel roof...(Alianza from UNC is helping with this project). And at the same time, we're showing the community, and again this is everybody not just Hispanics, but everybody that's willing to come. We're showing them that's, myself, how to do organic farming. And it doesn't have to be with compost, we're showing them with uh, rotten vegetables and worms. So we're trying to work on that small project... The farmworkers are the new growers of tomorrow. We don't expect a lot of people to come, but again, if we can bring five, six, that are really interested, that will really tell us that we have done and accomplished a lot.

Q: So do you think that small things like their own gardens, or, [Fito and Arturo] had their own chickens and stuff, like, personal possessions that connect them to the land, do you think that that's a part of them feeling

A: Yes, and I will tell you why. NC state, they came out with research that if you have one acre, one acre, you can manage to get a gross income of 15,000 dollars. Not something to get rich, but it's something where you and your family can live. Cause normally the lower income for poor families is 12,000. So 15 dollars out of once acre tells you a lot. Now, to get that money, it has to be organic. It has to be organic. Because in organic you get paid your money three times than what regular produce gets. And again last year we had classes where we've been teaching the community how to market that stuff. How to market, where to market, where to target. Uh, so it's been, on that we had a great impact with that so that was really good. So, at the same time we're showing people that, okay if you have another extra acre it's already proved to you if you're interested, it's a way to prove it to you on paper and people will come up, a corporal extension will come up, and teach you. Then, if you get another acre you're talking about 30,000 dollars, and now you can be your own boss. You can get up whenever you want to and you're just working your small little farm. So we've got some people who are really doing it.

Q: So you think some big themes are ownership, like having responsibility for your own thing, for yourself instead of having someone else responsible for you. And then, being able to feel as if you're contributing to the community around you

A: Yes, yes, in order words we're trying to show to the people is the impossible can be possible, and the small little things can mean a lot if you really put a hard work and effort and believe in it. And you have to stop being afraid. Of the challenge. And what I mean by that is like "I don't know, I've got this stable job, and I'm afraid of going there and putting my time into this will make me lose my job" and that's another thing they have to put time into it so they can try because if they don't really risk it, they're not ever gonna find out for sure if they really made it or not.

Q: So, a big thing, though, with all of this, though, is despite all of these contributions they may or may not be making, and money, they still won't have documentation.

A: When you're selling, they don't ask you for documentation. They just ask you if you've got good produce that looks pretty, and especially that there's no chemicals. Hospitals, restaurants, nursery homes, market will buy them.

Q: But you were talking about how sometimes when you're driving on the road you can be pulled off and asked for documentation

A: Yes, that is correct. But, that's when, then, you can find yourself a corporate, another corporation, a corporate organization that will say "well listen, we're dealing with small farmers. Can you come and pick up my stuff and you pay me right there. Cash money. Basically that's what they do right there is cash money. And, uh, that's one way. Another way is if you do, put signs where you can pick your own. Or you can make your own little stand outside your property and sell you own produce. I mean, there's different ways.

Q: So, you think that by expanding from being a farmworker for someone else it's also a way to have a legitimate establishment and not have to worry as much about documentation status?

A: Yes, because, the, the law. Okay. Normally the law will be really tough when the season is about to start or the season is about to end. That's when you need to be really cautious. But when not of you are starting it, you're okay. Now, second, you, as the farmworker, as the picker, you learn more from the farmer: what to pick what not to pick, what type of dirt is good, that you can cultivate or not cultivate. In other words, you're the one that's learning.

Q: Kind of like school

A: Yes, so you can put the skills into your own acreage. And it doesn't have to be something big. Let's say, small, you don't get rich, but you survive. And any money you get, that you manage to save up, then you can get a one-acreage, a two-acreage and you expand yourself. And there's a lot of markets these days there's the Hispanic market, the Hmong market, the Hindu market. You just have to focus on what you really want to do.

Q: So do you think that your kids, do you think that it's important that they understand how to

A: My kids, I'm going to explain to you the way that I was raised and brought up. My kids, especially the older ones. My kids, when they don't go to school I take them to the fields, not to watch, but I give them a bucket. Or whatever, whatever we're picking, I give them a bucket or a sack. And I say that "hey, go to work." My kids, they don't whine or cry, they go okay" I say "I'm doing this because I want you to know where you came from, your roots. I want you, so that way you can value, I want you to do this later on in the church when you're old enough, you don't offend a farmworker, you don't humiliate a farmworker, you understand where you come from and thanks to that farmworker you're wearing the clothes that you're wearing, you're eating what made you grow up. But I want you, later on in life, if I'm not here to defend it, I don't want anyone to come up to you and say 'hey you're a daddy's boy and you don't know how to do it' you can tell them, hey, I know how to do it. You will not be afraid or embarrassed to get a bucket." And that's what I teach my boys. If they don't do good in school, maybe I'm just strict, if I see a "B" I say "nuh uh! No more playstation" and I put the playstation away and say, okay. I like to hear good comments. For example, the teacher said "your son is really polite, is really helpful with the other students." Except for the middle one, the middle one is a bit, uh, he's not a bad kid, he's a bit into the flirty flirty. He got caught selling kisses for two pennies. Hahaha, I guess he got that from his grandaddy's side, but anyhow. That's what I'm trying to teach my boys, ah, value, to know where they come from. Not just because, again, daddy right now can buy them good clothes and good toys means that they're always going to be daddy's boys.

Q: So, do you think it's important that they ever return back to Mexico? Or

A: Not, not to return back, I mean

Q: Or to visit

A: That's up, that's up to them and I'm going to put it this way: we're four, three brothers and one sister in my family. Our hands, if you look at your fingers, they're different sizes. We cannot tell the pinky to do what the pointer wants to do. So if the pinky decided to be a farmer, then let him be a farmer, but if the pointer doesn't want to be on a farm even though he grew up to be a farmer, a picker, but he wants to be a lawyer, let him be a lawyer. So, to answer your question about going to Mexico, it's going to be pretty hard for me to tell them "hey, go back to Mexico because that's where me and your granddaddy came from." They might go to visit, but not really to Mexico. They might go where all the tourism goes, maybe to spend one week or two weeks. God knows, I don't know. But they're not going to see and treasure it the way we do. Me and daddy. They're going to see it as their regular vacation, that's it.

A: And to be honest with you. When I went back, those two times I went back, I never feel welcomed. And it's hard to say, I feel ashamed, but I just don't feel a home there anymore. I don't feel like, like you're welcomed, I feel more like a tourist. And the way life up there is, I guess because that time you lost from being over here, you're not adapted to it anymore, and you won't get adapted. So, no.

Q: Um, oh. So do you feel as if farm, working on farms, or agriculture, is a bigger part of, is more of your "roots" than Mexico is at this point then. Because you said that it's important for them to understand their roots and

A: It is. And, again, because, this is where, how we came. This is how we started our life. This is how we clothed ourselves this is how we managed to educate ourselves this is a way of living but it doesn't mean they have to be a replica of us but it's just a way of telling them where we came from. How hard it was for us to get a better, and how hard it was for us to provide them good clothes, an education, food, the opportunities that I didn't have. To treasure, to value all that stuff. It's just a way of teaching them. but it's not for them to be a farmworker.

Q: Alright, that's all the questions

A: Are you sure? You don't want to ask anything else?

Q: No, not unless you have anything else to say

A: Well, well, new page. Now since, let me tell you the way, I'm going to explain now the whole thing from where we started. Okay. Papa became a contractor in 1987, he was what we call a goat driver. And that has nothing to do with goats, it's a vehicle that picks up the oranges. Also another name, that's "crew leader" or "contractor." From there until 1990 daddy, uh, purchased his first land on highway 27 which is a big highway in Florida. And the reason we purchased the land was to leave them aside for the future. And whenever it's needed to sell them and with that money to purchase more land and something else with it, an investment.

A: 1994, uh, that time is when daddy managed to purchase his first 40 acres of citrus. And at the same time he managed to, uh, build four labor camps. But these labor camps were way different from the ones we were staying in when I was younger. They had AC, the whole building had AC, a heater, big space for the guys so they can have their own privacy, closets, kitchens were big enough and had refrigerators. So it was wonderful because I even managed to stay there sometimes. So it was pretty good.

Q: And bathrooms and stuff

A: Bathrooms: good; showers, private stalls, everything. We, daddy made a lot of difference compared to the labor camps we had been staying in. something that's really liveable. But every time the labor department would come over and do an inspection like they always do, they would say "we know your stuff is good" so they never, they never bothered us. They came one time only and from that time on, no more.

A: 1996, that's when daddy managed to purchase more land in Florida. By that time we had 200 acres. But still, daddy was still a contractor. He didn't see himself and a grower, a farmer yet. By that time there was 300-250 people.

Q: So you all would go to…would you, as a contractor, go back to mexico to recruit people to come?

A: No, the way the system works is, you know how we get all these people, back then in the 90's there were a lot of coyotes. So the coyotes would go find the contractors. How did they know who the contractors were? Well, let's say I have this person from Guatemala, well this person would contact his family and say "hey, guess what, there's work, you have to come over, the job's pretty good, the boss I'm working for is good and treats us fair[ly], he's not sticking it too us, on the contrary he's looking after us" and so on so on so on. So tell Julio, that's the man, to bring you over and my boss, contractor, will pay for you guys to come over here. Work a deal with the coyotes. So that's how the system worked back then.

Q: So contractors, I don't really understand the difference between contractors and growers, then.

A: Okay. Contractor is a crew leader. A crew leader used to be the leader of the pack

Q: So he still worked in fields

A: He still worked in the fields with them. He was the one that was picking up all the contracts from the farmer. That's why it became a contractor. He was making a contract for the farmer and saying "I'm going to pick up all the…"

Q: "these guys work for me"

A: "these guys work for me, you pay me and I pay them and I pick all your, whatever produce you have on your farm until the season finish and then I move on to another state" That's why many American farmers call them contractors. If you go to Florida, Texas, Georgia, California, they call them crew leaders. Here they call them contractors because you're making a contract with them. Whether it rains or shines you still have to pick up their stuff.

A: Okay, so, Julio would bring, and in that time the law was easy so it wouldn't be that bad, they'd bring in a small U-Haul, rental van, or a Sears van, bring twenty or thirty vans all piled in the back of them. Now, not over thirty would stay with that crew leader or contractor, maybe ten or fifteen. The other guys would have family in other states that would say "you bring them to my house, I'll pay you for them." Back then, they were charging $1,000 per head. Just to bring them from the border to whichever state. To cross them from Mexico to the border, that was $200. The Indians, the would put them with the Indians, and then the coyotes would go and pay them $50 for all those people they had there, and take them to them [their families]. That's how it would be done…Every coyote knows which one, so they'll be like "hey listen I'm going to NC" and "hey these guys are going to North Carolina, you pay me what they're going to pay me and take them" "Oh, okay" and boom boom boom boom, there was a lot of cash money going around.

A: So what happened was, Julio would end up leaving us those fifteen guys. We'd say "listen Julio, we don't have enough money, come back in two weeks, and I'll give you the money. But you leave them with me so that way you don't harass them you don't treat them bad, you don't do something with their families just because I didn't pay you. The guy doesn't pay you and walks away, it's on my responsibility." So that's how it works. And some of the guys, when they come to the crew leader, if the crew leader gives them crap, they'll escape. But see, what happens is the crew leader will know where they come from, they will charge their family in Mexico for the money that they owe. They'll take whatever cows they have to cover it, whatever produce they own to cover the expense. Steal one of their daughters. So, yes, it was crucial, it was harsh.

A: So, we never had this because all of our guys were treated equally and, uh, so that's how we managed to get a lot, lot, lot of people. And, papa, he never expected that. We expected to be small and, you know, twenty or thirty people. As time went on, uh, and in 2000 a lot happened.

A: In 2002 daddy managed to purchase a 1,000 acres. And, uh, that's where we got the blueberry farm. In total we got 1,048 acres. And, uh, daddy and I never paid attention to that. By that time daddy was already out of, and god knows where, we managed to become from a contracor to a farmer. IN florida, that's where dad mananged to rent a big packing house. And, rent 400 acres, besides the 200 acres, 400 acres to start planting vegetables. And in the year 2000 citrus was going pretty bad, so we managed, what we did, on those 200 acres, we killed everything else, and what we planted was watermelons. 100 acres seedless, 100 acres with seeds. Watermelons. And that 400 acres we planted 100 acres of tomatoes, and the rest was bell pepper, squash, zucchini, and greenbeans.

A: 2002 everything was going smooth. The people he had back then, only about 10 people stayed with us, and those ten people daddy managed to give them a good position. To be supervisors, to be tractor drivers, to be in charge of the packing-house, of when the 18 wheelers cam to pick up the stuff, to be in charge of the new generation of contractors. Because back then, the new generation of contractors were the old coyotes. They were no longer bringing the people to the "old dinosaurs," that's what we were called back then the old crew leaders, instead they became the contractors. So then the people that were bringing them were bringing to themselves to work directly. Uh, since then, then the border was a lot harder, now the coyote was charging the guys $1,100. To get them from mexico was $500 instead of $200 dollars. Again, we never got involved in that, it was just what the guys were telling us…

A: But keep in mind, in that time, daddy and my mom, they were never there with us. Neither of the, because they were always at work, work, work. They never went to my highschool graduation; they never went to see us when we were playing sports. They were never there with us on our happy birthday parties. They were always work. By that time I was helping dad already, running a few crews. Taking care of the, the crew leaders and all that. And that's where I met my boy's mama, at the packing-house. I mean, I met a lot of women like that, though. I was looking for someone who was, that was really, to like you and love you for who you are, not for what you're….and that's where that ends, and where that story picks up, from the other question about the kids. Uh.

A: In 2004, we were doing really well, but it was never a family feeling. We were always coming home, never talking about the day, we were like strangers. Uh, we never even cared how you feeling and what you were thinking. In 2004 I managed to purchase my, a house. A full-blown concrete house with a porch, swimming pool in the back. And that year I was 24 yearls old. Again, since I was living in labor camps I was living way different, I was mature way too early. I never spent a night with friends I never went with friends to go to a movie theatre. My only enjoyment was just playing sports in school. My other two brothers, on the contrary, they were more, uh, they didn't live the same life I did they were more regular life, normal life. They went to friends' houses, stuff like that, and my sister was the same way. At first I was a little mad at that, because, anyhow. So we were living pretty well. We were wealthy; we were one of the wealthiest Hispanic families in four counties. We had, well they said, money up the butt. Uh, to the point that, uh, okay if we go to this auction, we buy this truck and this tractor. If I want to change a pickup truck I just call Ford and say "I don't want this truck anymore, get me a new one, I want this, this, this." To that point, to how spoiled we were, to how much rotten we were. And we were always thinking money money money money, have to make more money, how to make more money, but we were forgetting the most important thing: family.

A: In 2004 something happened that changed our lives. My smaller brother passed away, sixteen years old. A lost bullet hit him on the head. But it didn't go through or anything, it just, you know. Right here (on the side). And the bad thing about it, they went to see an uncle of mine, and uh, the bad thing about it he died in daddy's arms, and mama was right there. And, uh, the ambulance came real late. Papa managed to revive him with CPR, but the guys were, they were racial, they didn't want to touch him because he was bleeding, didn't want to get infected. I mean, he was a sixteen-year-old kid. So by the time they went back to where the ambulance was, picked up their gloves, my brother had already passed away. And then my dad understood that the world here is harsh. That even though you have money there's still a lot of discrimination going on. My mama went crazy. By that time I was at the mall, that's when we had our second child, Reuben. I had a phone call from dad that said "hey, you need to come" it was a three hour drive, I said "what happened" he said "you just need to come, your brother is gone" and I thought when he said that, I still remember that every day is his birthday, I thought he meant like, with some chick or ran away. But you always get that feeling inside. And, I went to pick up my brother and my sister and, I knew. And all the way I started crying, and my sister, she started crying, she said "what happened" we used to call my brother Louie from that cartoon, Louie Anderson, I don't know if you remember it, and I said "well I think Louie just passed away." There was silence. That three-hour drive, I made it to a one hour and thirty minute drive. How? Well, I don't know. The ambulance was already taking my brother to the funeral place. Me and my brother were, uh, I didn't lose control, I don't know why. My brother and my sister did. So, I still went up there and saw my brother and he was cold. But he left with a smile, so I know he didn't suffer. Mama was, my mama was gone. My grandmamma came and picked her up and took her. My uncle was destroyed my dad was destroyed and they put a lawsuit with the ambulance people and also a lawsuit with the sheriff department because they were accusing my uncle as the one who shot him. You see the thing was my uncle had a divorce and that old lady was dating one of the sheriffs, and he didn't like my uncle. It could have been that we were the only Hispanics in ___ with a lot of land, or him, a lot of horses, a lot of land and so on, so on. So they're always trying to find a way to, uh, like anywhere else, to find a way to find something to say "hey, you're corrupted" or "you're laundry money" or anything. So, back then, my uncle had a few law cases with the law and he managed to win. He had a few lawsuits with the county so he managed to win. So when daddy, when daddy was trying to do that, it took a lot of money but, since they didn't like us, they just said that there was no hard evidence, there was not a case and so on.

A: From that point daddy said I don't have time to think. The land that we were renting, it still had some of the mortgages, we were still owing them, we were running close to 400 people at the packing house, they all depended on us. Contracts with Wal-Mart, Winn Dixie when Winn Dixie was still Winn Dixie, Anderson, uh, daddy said "you know what, tell everybody, go home. Auction the place, auction everything. I don't want to know anything." So on 2005 we were able to auction off everything. Anything that would have cost us close to $80,000 we auctioned for $10,000. So we came up a little bit short. That time, uh, mama, didn't want to come out of the house. Their house was empty, there was no more laughter, there was not more, that joy, there was nothing. That house is where we all grew up and were raised. I came to a point, I said "you know what, I'm going to sell my house" and back then the housing market was still pretty good, so I sold my house. So, the fame of the Estevez family was still there but a lot of people who had a lot of envy of us, the old dinosaurs, that hadn't managed to, uh, I guess get the same luck we did, with the same opportunity, they just came to the house to, you know, laugh, "once you get up there the hard part is to stay up there." Even my family, my mama's side of the family, there were some uh..., and that's where we understood the only family we had was just us. The only friends we had were just us. The only people we could depend on was just us.

A: In 2006 that's when we decided to come up here, we said "you know what, let's go to North Carolina" and I talked to father rafa. And I said "father rafa, this is what is going on, my mom is going crazy, my dad can't think straight, my sister decided she wanted to go to the army, my brother doesn't want to finish college." My, uh, we were not married but we were living together, we had Johnnie, things were not going well, because she was used to living a good life, good house, when we came here we came to a crappy old trailer that was at the blueberry farm, so all of us were all piled in. And, I always told daddy and her that it was just going to be temporary it was not like they were going to stay there forever. Until we get out mind and bearing and everything. So Father Rafa came up and helping mama and daddy and all of us, to go to therapy. So he helped, I don't know how Father managed to get in contact with this person, uh, they didn't charge us anything. Father Rafa took care of that, I don't know if he paid them, until then I still don't know. Mama kept going and Daddy kept going. And I'm not going to lie to you, whenever I was alone I wasn't made out of stone and that's when I let it all loose. But whenever I was in front of them I had to show them that I was strong. My sister, um, she, in the army, she became second lieutenant. My brother managed to finish with a associates degree in marketing. So, I had the opportunity to go back to school but with the problems I had with the laws with the relations in the school, I never got my highschool diploma but I did get enough credits, and just because I was in this state and they were giving me four classes, and this other state was giving me six classes, whatever they had, they didn't count. I had to go back and forth and they didn't count all that. They sat me down and said "listen" and I still remember that they said "listen, you better be grateful they're going to get credit, but you're not going to get your highschool diploma. You're still going to be there with your classmates but you're not going to get your diploma"

Q: You got your GED?

A: I haven't given myself time to get my GED. I lost hope in that. It got me, uh, I was depressed. Depressed, but because, uh, I couldn't get it but depressed because it wasn't fair. They put my through a lot of crap and a lot of promises but I still didn't get what I proved to them I should. It brought my self-esteem down. Til today I want to go back to school, my dream is to be a lawyer, still is. But I'm trying to get myself financially sustainable, then I can leave the farm, go on to school and get my GED. Uh, a lot of people from NC A&T university, I met a Dr. McCanon, we became good friends and he said "listen, if you want to come, I can help you with financials, you just have to choose one of the agricultural degrees so think about it and I'll help you all the way." Another person from Florida, Florida State University, named Dr. Straughn, said "listen, if you want to come, you've got a lot of potential, help you out the whole way." So I've got a lot of opportunities.

A: Going back to the story, so, what happened, was, as time went on the blueberries came into production. Uh, mom and daddy managed already to be okay, daddy came back to his senses, my sister, this coming up month is going to be her last year of the contract so she's coming back home. Uh, she's a different person now. My brother got in love with a chick, that I don't really know, but you have to support him, you know he's the only brother I got. My kids, well, since that time, she left us, she did not like going through our hard times. I said, "well, listen, when I was born and raised and before we got where we were, I learned how to be poor. And I never forgot how to be poor because I never humiliated nobody, there's nobody that would really tell me that I humiliated them because I used to be up here. on the contrary, even though was up here, I was still help people, charity, giving them money, helping them out. But she said, "when you were down there, none of those people were helping out, with you or your family, why are you still helping people out? What are you trying to get?" and I told her, well listen, it's just that I was a migrant person and I know how it feels, and sometimes you feel like a superhero that way so I'm going to help them out, asking for nothing in return. And that's why I'm doing it. It's not because I want something in return but, at least, when my time comes, the big man will say "listen, you did a good deed." And at the same time it's opening more doors, more relationships with other people. And that's how I got involved with other organizations. I guess, people, the word got spread out and people come and "would you like to be the co-chair of this" and "would you like to be the co-chair of this" and so on and so on. And so that's how I got so much involved in multiple organization more political and I guess since granddaddy has been political and daddy has been political we just have something in our genes that, whether you want it or not, is political. Now, when I'm trying to do work it's hard because I'm having some hard times with the FSA (Farm Service Agency) here in North Carolina again, because, (SIGH), we're the only Hispanic farmers with a lot of land, they don't want to give us a loan to expand our business and start back again. So, we've been fighting with FSA for the past five years. For justice, against discrimination, with appeals through appeals, visits to Washington, visits to the main personnel in the USDA (US Department of Agriculture). And through all that, is, to learn more about how the system works. And maybe it's not the correct work but the sad part is that I've been living on that, I've been able to help out other people in other states but I can not help out my own self and my own family. So, that's the sad part. I can help people but I cannot help my own. Maybe I'm not at that point yet to be helping my own self after I accomplish what we want. Maybe I'm missing something since I'm always on the run I'm not paying enough attention. Um, and again, thanks to that I got more involved with Father Rafa, to the organizations, I've been giving more funds to the CMFF. It isn't much, but it's something…

Made in the USA
Columbia, SC
12 December 2018